My Little Casa

The fun and unique experience of buying a property in the wilds of Portugal

By Lee Middlenam

For anyone looking to follow their dream

Copyright

Self-published in 2018

Copyright © Lee Middlenam 2017

Lee Middlenam has asserted rights as an author of this work under the global copyright laws where no part of this work can be reproduced in any form or by any means without permission from the publisher.

ISBN: 9781980958789

Table of Contents

Copyright 2

Preface 5

1. The Dream 7
2. The Unknown..12
3. Deal Done..16
4. The Exchange..19
5. The Recovery..24
6. Completion...28
7. The Return..33
8. Children's Time...38
9. Week of Reckoning.....................................41
10. Walk Time...44
11. Festival Fun...48
12. Pop-up Restaurant Experience.................51
13. Final Discovery Day 54
14. Operation Stealth 56
15. Next Day Arrives......................................59
16. Mystical Sintra Experience 61
17. Quinta da Regaleira Time 65
18. September Days 68
19. Porto Covo Beach Day 73
20. Best Kept Secret 76
21. Secret Pond 79

22. Shellfish Gold 83

23. DIY Day 87

24. Final Beach Day 90

25. Alentejo Reflections 94

26. The Short One 97

27. Pre-Christmas Tan 101

28. The Unknown Tour 105

29. Final Furlong 107

30. Crossroads 111

Acknowledgements 115

Helpful Tips 116

Helpful Links 118

Preface

If you have opened this book, it possibly means that you have dreamt of buying a nice little holiday home in Portugal or any other place far away from the hustle and bustle of life in the busy cities around the globe. What does it take to actually go through with it? What sort of crazy person agrees to buy before visiting and what would be the reality of buying a property in the isolated villages in the warm harsh plains of the Alentejo?

Every person has their own unique thoughts but why do some people turn their dreams a reality? What sort of person does it take to go from a fear of flying to making an instant decision to by a property in a country, without even visiting the location, where locals speak a different language?

My alarm went off at the crack of dawn, and I struggled to get up and out as planned. I settled for slowly waking up prior to gathering my newly acquired fishing gear and heading out of the door In this book I have created a brief guide of the steps leading up to that special purchase. But rather than focus on the legal and complex procedures I have documented real experiences, in real time as they happened, writing possibly the first book in the world with my trusted travel companion, the iPhone SE.

It was never my intention to write a book, but the process wasn't all plain sailing as I encountered various issues during the experience. In one short year and quite a few flights to sunnier climates later, my simple blog turned into something far bigger than I ever imagined.

Throughout my wonderful life-changing experience, you'll get a sense of fun as I proceed with my journey, through the research stage, to completion. Things really start to gain momentum as we travel through the amazingly rich and tranquil lands in the Alentejo area of sun drenched Portugal.

For all those considering such a life changing and magical adventure this will hopefully encourage you to follow your dreams.

It's not all glitz and glam, in fact, it's the complete opposite, but sometimes in life you have to take an opportunity like I did. I would never want to go through life wishing I'd done something special; I'd much rather be the one telling my grandchildren of the moment I made a difference to those around me.

So many people will doubt your ability and dismiss your dreams, but smile in the face of adversity and use their negativity to fuel that desire to succeed; the end result will be a profound thought of contentment.

1. The Dream

I've rarely thought the same way as other people possibly due to a lack of intelligence, perhaps, or just a lack of skills in other areas. But I've always had a keen eye for investment opportunities, despite lacking in funds. Unfortunately, or fortunately in this case, I'm someone who likes to take a risk and once I'm on a mission to make something happen there's very little to stop me. So when one morning I made a sudden decision to buy a house in Portugal, it was going to happen and very little would prevent me from moving forward. Easy, right?

Only factors beyond my control have ever held me back, so making a decision to invest in international property was surprisingly quite easy. Well, it seemed that way from the outside. The reality was actually a little different. Rather than making a snap decision, I used my skills as a building specialist in the UK to research potential property hotspots that would fit my minimal investment budget and to gather data on potential future hotspots post-Brexit. In the one year since my purchase, the price of property has shot up and a 36% gain is forecast for 2017 with no sign of any change on the horizon.

So what did I look for? First, after twelve months of searching I needed to be realistic about the amount of time I would be able to allocate to a large project. In one fell swoop, I cut by a whopping 50% my slightly larger than life list of online properties around the globe. I was also forced to abandon my plans for a Hungarian dream home and vineyard; letting my head snatch back my heartstrings.

Gone was my passionate dream of a large mountain property accompanied by a number of outbuildings to house my quad bikes.

This reduced my property list by another 30%, and in turn left a selection of twenty properties. The decision was made and the winner went to Portugal. During my research I discovered some of the finest unspoilt coasts in Europe, stunning protected national parks, great infrastructure and wonderful people and if that was not enough, I discovered some of the lowest property prices in developed Europe. What a great idea I thought. Only a little more than an hour's drive from the Algarve was the sun-baked Alentejo region, surrounded by wild rolling hills, cascading streams and free roaming cattle taking refuge around the vast array of olive and fruit trees, while other animals grazed on the open plains that made up the amazing landscape.

I decided to take a little trip to Faro eventually finding a small town just east of Albufeira in the old fishing town of Olhos de Agua where local waiters dismissed my research as a distant pipe dream. They explained in their broken English that any property purchase would be impossible for my planned investment of 22,000 euros. *Nao sy, Mr English, no dealio for 22k, not possibalio*! Mmm well, Mr Waiter, Mr English believes in the impossible and does not give up. *Esta bem* in my best Portuguese.

I was now more determined than ever, and after speaking to a variety of estate agents all politely dismissing my plans I decided to look at the next area on the borders of the Algarve and found an area of Portugal virtually unknown to most UK citizens: the Beja strip in the Alentejo region, which runs parallel with the Algarve. Suddenly my business head clicked into overdrive and I decided that was the place. My gut feeling sent shivers through my body and at that point there was no other choice. My long list was then depleted to two. A sale had been agreed on one property the day after my decision, which left one more possibility – what a great choice considering it was only a one-hour drive from the Algarve. This was ideal. A new Ikea store and designer village were near completion, and the hugely impressive expansion of Faro airport recently taken over by the French had boosted the area. These developments were creating some 3,000 full time jobs, which really excited my taxi driver, even if he was a little moany about the increased charges for his airport access while thankfully receiving his tip. '*Much obrigado*, sir,' he said as he jumped back into his luxury Mercedes taxi driving off into the sunset never to be seen again.

    I then had a quick reality check. Was it the Brit's abroad experience I was looking for with a one-bedroom studio in Albufeira or was it possibly something slightly different to take me away from my busy life in Clapham in south-east London? That night I studied my second-hand map of Portugal eventually finding Beja airport. I discovered a lovely little coastal location by the name of Vila Nova de Milfontes, which is favoured among our EU cousins and locals alike. This place is known to be one of the choices for the city-dwelling Lisbonites to escape their busy life, similar to Londoners who head to Brighton. It was a genuinely beautiful town with attractive national parks, rolling hills, roaming cattle and stunning unspoilt west coast beaches. The little town had a great selection of shops and services and a vibrant, small arty town atmosphere, an ideal holiday spot for Banksy. This was made more attractive by the whitewashed stone buildings mounted on top of attractive cobble stone platforms, with loads of quality restaurants and snack bars all offering lovely food, great service and amazing value for money.

Okay, now I had my lovely little coastal town not far from Beja airport and that night I discovered that there was talk about operating more commercial flights although some planning and infrastructure discussions needed to be resolved; this meant great investment potential. I looked at the map, judged about forty-five minutes inland and eventually came to an area by the name of Vale de Santiago, which appeared to be a traditional sleepy village consisting of only 500 families. Now the real magical experience would begin.

Once back in the UK and with my new discovered knowledge I excitedly booted up my iPad and a gift from God appeared on my screen in the form of a quaint little structure, furnished throughout for the amazing price of 27,000 euros. I was certain at that point that it would be mine, but for what price? Within twenty minutes I'd made contact with an estate agent with the very un-Portuguese name of Tim, who immediately came back to confirm the property was available to view on the Sunday morning. I couldn't help thinking it was all too easy. Maybe there was some sort of Portuguese mafia repeatedly selling the same property as part of an international money-laundering cartel. But in reality it was a friendly estate agent named Tim who was originally from Holland but now happily settled in Portugal, learning the local lingo to add to his English-speaking war chest! *Olá*, Tim.

I then made what some might consider a cheeky offer of 25,000 euros to an already keenly priced property. Thinking back to my original plans, it would need to include all the furniture to prevent too many trips to get it ready for the family while giving me a unique selling point if I decided to sell. And no threat of me having to spend endless days building flat pack furniture in the midday sun with Portuguese instructions to add to the fun; not a great thought considering I didn't speak a word of Portuguese.

I made it clear I was a deadly serious cash buyer, and I would be looking to complete the deal as soon as possible. The offer was agreed, no doubt with a little reluctance from the seller as I hadn't even visited the area, which some would consider high risk. Twenty-four hours later I found myself booking my first international flight on my own and ordering my hire car. I was lucky to have my new buddy Tim to take care of the hotel reservation, which came complete with a huge parrot and a lively talking one at that. Luckily we seemed to get on quite well.

A journey in to the unknown is just like any other journey but comes with no expectations placed upon you from the people who become part of it.

2. The Unknown

Just to recap, I had never booked a flight myself in my life; I had never driven on the 'incorrect' side of the road and I certainly never imagined that I would take a road trip alone in a foreign land.

While agreeing to buy the property and unintentionally putting myself under a lot of sudden pressure, I managed to grab a real bargain on the flights paying only £29.99 to fly out and not much more to fly back home. Wow, that's less than a train journey in the UK I excitedly explained to my family and friends. I downloaded an annual insurance for hire car cover and booked a great little bargain in the form of Fifi the Fiat at only £5 a day. So far so good.

The day before leaving the UK for Portugal, my new homeland, I was quite excited and had no idea what I was getting myself into, which really was part of the fun. I imagined the mafia waiting for me at the property with a horse's head as a welcome gift, but thankfully my mind was playing tricks and it turned out to be just my friendly estate agent Tim.

All through the week I had been in contact with Tim who worked for the brilliant Remax network, a fully approved agent with various legal obligations, which gave me a feeling of security. I guesstimated that if I was to leave London at 4 a.m. I should arrive at Vale de Santiago at midday, allowing for lunch and refreshments, and a little walk around the village to get to know the locals prior to my meeting with Tim.

Having checked in at the airport, I was on my way to Portugal. I wasn't really thinking about the process but simply focusing on just getting to the property, agreeing a deal and sitting on my terrace drinking sangria in the sun, forgetting about the reality of rushing around checking out the area and loads of meetings in order to get the deal done.

Eventually I arrived at Faro at 9.30 a.m., giving me loads of time to negotiate a free car upgrade but getting stung with the gold insurance on the car to save me handing over a £1200 deposit, which then called in to question why I took out a third party insurance. We live and learn.

The trip from the airport took me through winding mountain roads, along miles of wild dirt tracks through the open plains. I honked my way through various groups of goats and sheep wandering around the wild countryside oblivious to the poor tired Englishman stuck behind them.

What I'd loved on my recent trips to Portugal was that everyone in the Algarve seemed to speak brilliant English. I was soon to find out, while stopping off at the service station, that these rules might not apply as you tour up country. Luckily I had my little pointy finger with me, and my pointing skills became invaluable, almost as good as my faithful TomTom1 satnav previously updated some ten years prior to the trip, hmmm there was something I missed. A big fat software update, along with translation software, towropes and a Portuguese language course would have been great as well.

Getting to my first destination was a real pleasure. At the local service station I pointed my way to a flatbread chicken sandwich and a lovely ice-cold coke that I enjoyed in the morning sun. I'd travelled a long way and didn't know what to expect on my journey ahead, so I felt a quick visit to the little boys' room would be appropriate. Then it hit me. In rural Portugal, the service stations have holes in the ground, which they call toilets. But I was becoming even more excited by my new life in a simple culture away from the trappings of the inner city madness of London.

After navigating relatively empty motorways, passing through mountains, over rivers and creeks and various historic castles I eventually zigzagged my way to a small dirt track in the middle of nowhere. It was at that point I wondered if I was having a midlife crisis or just going totally bonkers. Fighting the negativity, I decided my actions were fairly normal and continued on my quest.

I managed to get held up a few times by animals grazing along the side of the road as I entered the village. I waved to the local farmers tending to their fields, '*Olá*, farmer man'. As I drove into the village I could see in the distance a stunning whitewashed church in the classic Portuguese style and was pleased to have made it alive. I parked in the village and was surprised that I was the only person walking around. As I walked to explore the church, the bells started to ring as the minute hand reached 12 o'clock. I'd arrived at my destination at the exact time that I'd planned.

I walked around the village for a while, booking from the outside I discovered the café down the road was closed, in fact, all the local shops appeared to be closed and there was a lack of people in the village. Little did I realise at that the village had shut for lunch. I saw Tim arrive in his super sports estate car ready to show me the property. Tim was great, there was no pressure, and he was more than happy to answer all my questions; you could tell he had a real passion for helping people.

Entering the house was really a formality before I agreed the deal. Tim opened the multi-locking door, which led to the hall with the original 1920's ceramic floor tiles. Beyond that was a stunning little courtyard where I discovered loads of fresh green and red grapes in my own little casa. Then I worked my way up to the podium level to look at the stunning view of the countryside, which consisted of steep grass hills littered with lively sheep and goats grazing while little bells draped from their fluffy necks rang out across the valleys.

I failed to realise at first that there would be an outside bathroom, but this just added to the romantic dream of a traditional little Portuguese village home. It was very likely that I would definitely progress with the purchase but I told Tim that I would sleep on it overnight. You should never seem too keen with these things.

We set off for the unspoilt town of Vila Nova de Milfontes, which sits beside the stunning west coast. I followed Tim, my chief tour guide, to the hotel where he booked me in before making his way back to the office.

3. Deal Done

As we walked into the reception, I was delighted to discover a great host in the form of an extremely large talking parrot who I aptly named Ronaldo, due to his pretty boy looks but slightly irritating conversation skills. I was delighted by the attractive little hotel room, which took me back to 70s London with antique furniture and basic conveniences. At 2 a.m., Ronaldo suddenly screamed, '*Obrigado, bom dia,*' and delivered an amazing language course, preparing me for my journey ahead. I'd be lying if I said I wasn't tempted to sneak him in my hand luggage, but with the airline's reduction in baggage size I felt it might not be such a great idea.

That night while laying on my spring-loaded mattress, I thought about the additional costs for white goods and other household items that we often take for granted. Then I thought about health and safety upgrades and more trips that would need to be made to complete the process. So, I decided to try my luck and slightly reduce the offer knowing that I was on a very strict budget, however, this could have meant losing the house. I thought it would be worth asking based on the pound tumbling in value due to Brexit on the day I agreed to buy, which was just my luck, but I wasn't going to let that stop me.

The next day I arranged a second visit before making my final decision. By this time the angry seller had rejected my latest offer, so I needed to quickly work out minimal upgrade costs to see if it would still fit in with my extremely tight budget. Luckily, by the time the works were carried out, my estimation of 2,500 euros ended up being extremely close to the value that I envisaged.

I did some research on crime, historic buildings, beaches and infrastructure, and I found only positive reports so I told Tim that I was happy to proceed. It was an incredible feeling. It took me back to the first property I purchased in the UK, a feeling that lasted just over ten minutes at which point my stomach started twitching and hunger took over.

I went out explore the local town and surrounding beaches, and treated myself to a lovely meal in a stunning restaurant next door to the hotel. Everything on the menu was locally produced. There was an amazing selection of Alentejo style bread drizzled in oil, a side dish of freshly picked olives and a lovely Portuguese style stew to build up my energy levels. All of this was complemented with a glass of green vino, which was particularly pleasing. And the service was great. Eventually I staggered out of the restaurant, unfortunately not due to the wine but the volume of local food I consumed, an extremely happy Englishman, albeit a slightly rounded one.

Tim and I met the following day and I opened my first Portuguese bank account, which was exciting. We went over the entire process until it was crystal clear, and Tim printed guide copies of the expected contracts for me. I jumped into Fifi, my hire car, and said farewell to Tim, until the next time.

It had been a fairly hectic period and made me realise that it wasn't just a quick flight to sign a contract, which was what I hoped for, but would require far more work and involve loads of flying to secure my destiny. I started to wonder how to explain to my partner that I might have to make frequent visits to complete the deal. I wasn't sure if she would accept how hard this would be for me – any property deal can be extremely stressful and I have the hotel and restaurant bills to prove it.

I was still busy searching for other properties to add to my portfolio, but in the months following the Brexit referendum, there appeared to be a rather large decrease in the low budget properties. It was clear that although Brexit was being negotiated it didn't affect the international market as demand was now becoming greater than supply. From my experience in property, I guesstimated at least a 30% increase over the next year, although this would be offset by a possible 30% tax on profits, but money was never a factor in this latest adventure in the unknown lands of the Alentejo.

I felt really pleased with what I'd achieved under some difficult circumstances, but I had always remained focused and nothing could stop me in my quest of fulfilment in this latest chapter of my life. At least I didn't think so.

4. The Exchange

With the transaction now in progress, it was hard not to doubt my decision. But rather than spending too long on the negatives I remained fully focused on the positives. Back in the UK it was time to face reality; I was about to buy a property in a foreign country, but it would be an amazing experience for my children so nothing would stop me.

With the funds safely transferred from my account to Remax, off I flew to Alentejo again. I now had a good idea of the natural protected beaches as well as the arable landscapes and wide open plains and there no doubt in my mind that this would happen. I booked into my favourite little hotel with Ronaldo still present on the front desk, squealing all kinds of Portuguese phrases, but this time he seemed slightly less eccentric perched on his cage and I think he was all talked out, luckily for me.

At my next meeting with Tim, we checked the money and I struggled to log in to my bank account in the UK, which was a real pain. After a forty-five minute phone call to the UK I was logged in, the money had been transferred and would hit the Remax bank account after the weekend.

During the day I decided to try out Furnas Beach, the lovely little quiet beach opposite Vila Nova de Milfontes. It sits on the opposite side of the mouth to the powerful and historic Mira River where the river and the Atlantic come face to face. It creates amazing tidal surges evident by the constant ripples over and around the sand banks, leaving no doubt about the challenges of attempting to swim this section of the Mira.

It was fairly hot but I had limited time for lying around on the soft golden sand. Knowing that I still had a number of items to take care of, I headed to one of the long tree-lined tracks, past the various touring vans, and was shocked to notice a large dilapidated coloured house at the end of the beach. A few locals were patiently collecting their seafood offerings on the beach not too far from it. Being slightly inquisitive and because my job as a surveyor leaves me more interested in buildings than most people I decided to explore.

I parked and wandered down to the beach and a lady appeared from the structure along the beach front, so I assumed she was with the other locals who were patiently collecting their evening meal. I walked towards the people who were on their knees digging franticly with their bare hands before the tide came, trying to get the cockles embedded below the surface of the soft but saturated sand. I watched for a bit and after a while started to go back to the car, but my legs were now beginning to cramp with all the walking and the heat. So I made my way up the little dusty dirt track towards the derelict building on the way, wondering how such an amazing building could have been left to fall in to such a state of disrepair.

As I got closer, I noticed the lady who I saw earlier coming from the house now sitting in her car. She appeared to be getting dressed, which I was more than a little embarrassed about, but as I worked my way past the car along the little dirt track the shock turned to a horror as I realised this was no lady; it was a transvestite. My heart was now pounding with shock as she/he looked up and in a deep Portuguese voice greeted me, '*Boa Tarde,*' while changing clothes. I was down a little quiet road on my own and in a place I knew nothing about, so I quickly made my way back to the car. Upon my return to my trusted old metal friend, I quickly locked the doors and my shock turned to laughter. I could see the funny side and decided to give him/her a pet name called Tina. I put my quest for photos on hold and would once all occupants, including Tina, had departed.

That evening I planned to return, hoping that Tina would be long gone, to try to get some great photos of the castle during the stunning sunset hours. Just as I got there the sun was about to disappear and the deep orange sunset dropped beyond the horizon, unfortunately I was a little too slow to react as it dropped so quickly, preventing me from getting that prize winning photo that I was keen to send back home in order to sell my dream.

After a day of various meetings such as the tax office, trip to bank and others were out of the way I had a little time to go back to my room and chill for a bit prior to rushing out during the sunset hours. I was eager not to miss the opportunity this time.

I headed out into the cool summer air towards Odemira along the tree-lined roads and decided to visit as many beaches as possible. I started at the one furthest afield which was a lovely fishing spot with a thin path zigzagging down the cliffs; all the little fishing boats were coming in with the day's catch. There was a large group of about twenty wild cats patrolling the area in search of leftover food, very wary of any intruders or foreign visitors and they hissed at me as I walked towards them so I decided to maybe avoid a quick stroke.

This made some fantastic photos and it was so peaceful watching the wild cats play with each other; it made me really appreciate the country, which in turn made my decision seem even more right. Marching back up the hill to Fifi, I noticed pipes drilled into the slate rocks, which had spring water trickling out and glistening in the evening sun. I couldn't resist a quick slurp and face wash much to the amazement the twenty or so curious wild cats who were perched on the exposed slate ridges that formed the cliffs. After taking a few more photos, I drove back up the little dirt track packed with touring caravans by this time, and on to my next destination.

The sun was going down so I rushed off to my final beach of the day intending to get that sought after snap of the castle, anxiously hoping that the sun wouldn't disappear before I got there, and also hoping that Tina had packed up for the day once again.

Driving down the track, I was delighted to see that Tina had long gone from her unofficial commercial residence. Along the road there was a lone parked touring vehicle just past the little coloured house. The sun was still slightly showing over the horizon so I thought this would be perfect to capture the castle from the house looking towards the sun.

As I drove further down the track the sun was disappearing minute by minute so I decided to abandon my plan and go to the carpark where the tourer was parked, intending to spin around and make my way back up the dusty coastal path. As I drove down I found out that the road had finished and with a loud thump, I'd successfully managed to grind my vehicle skilfully in the beach true adventurer style!

This was when I realised that danger comes in many forms but with nature we are all at its mercy.

5. The Recovery

To recap, I was stuck firmly in the sand, but it wasn't so appealing in the dark, not far from the area that I discovered Tina negotiating her services. My memory was forced to back track to the earlier events and I started to worry, imagining a mad axe murderer hiding out in their tourer not far from where I was stuck in the sand. Cape Fear suddenly fixed into my brain so I relied on my best weapon to date: my little fingers remaining tightly crossed.

I felt extremely anxious but refused to give up, so in true Top Gear style I planned my escape and came up with loads of genius ideas to dig myself free. I increased traction on the tyres embedded deeply in the sand, trying not to disturb the parked touring van, which may come complete with the Cape Fear guy busy munching on his ounce of flesh. At least I had my phone.

After about forty minutes it was dark, and it was clear that I was out of my depth. I had no choice but to approach the vehicle like a lost schoolboy. As I shuffled along the sand to the van, I discovered a slightly older couple about to tuck in to a gorgeous-looking dessert. I gave a huge sigh of relief, and tried not to make it too obvious that I was frightened in any way shape or form, even though this was far more scary than the streets of London at night time.

I felt my mobile phone vibrate gently and slowly switch off as the battery died. But that wasn't a problem; I had my new friends. Upon explaining the situation I realised that they was every bit as scared of me as I was of them until and we attempted to make conversation. They were from France and spoke no English at all; add to this the fact I was totally unable to speak French, it wasn't exactly a match made in heaven.

After a little while I managed to direct them to my vehicle with my new pointing skills, which seemed to work well even. Once my eyes got used to the darkness it didn't take rocket science to work out that I was totally bogged down in the sand with the engine completely buried up to a third, which I was able to assess using the Frenchman's high-powered torch. 'Oh dear. Once again it just gets better,' I said to them as they shook their heads.

So there was me, the Frenchman and his wife all shovelling away like warriors attempting imaginative ways to free my car. They knew that if I was stuck then there was no way for them to get out either. After an hour we were still digging and the negative vibes started to really kick in. Would I be forced to leave the car? How would I get back? What would happen if I didn't make it in the morning? Would I lose my deposit? Failure was never an option at that point.

I was now franticly digging with my bare hands, which were extremely sore and blistered, so we decided to wander down the lonely dirt tracks in search of assistance from any other touring vehicle that might have still been there, but discovered that they had all long gone. Just as we were about to give up a gift from God arrived in the form of a battered old camper van limping down the dirt track and out of this van jumped a lovely Spanish couple and, guess what, they didn't speak English or French.

My survival instincts really kicked in. As we all worked tirelessly to free my car out of the sand, I made it clear that I was very sorry that the UK was leaving the EU and worked hard to convince them we made a great team. We were all now smiling, accepting this as an unexpected experience that we would no doubt be talking about in years to come.

We now had another vehicle perfectly placed but we really needed a rope. Out of nowhere, the French couple pulled out a large survival kit that included more torches, ropes and shovels that would have been extremely useful three hours earlier and we started to free my car, laughing our way through the recovery process.

We dragged my old faithful free without getting the third vehicle stuck, which was a bonus. What a joyous moment. I expressed my heartfelt thanks and reached into my wallet to tip my hosts only to find I had spent my last cash on the meal earlier that day. After multiple handshakes and double cheek kisses, I disappeared back in to the darkness to grab some extremely well earned sleep.

I awoke somewhat low on energy and arrived in the lovely little financial town of Odemira to greet the sellers Riora and Dimitri along with Tim. To my delight the sellers were really nice with a few good stories to tell.

The exchange was very straightforward and was done with the estate agents in the Notary's office, which is a critical part of the process as they are trained to ensure that no dishonest transactions take place from either party. This consisted of running through the contract with Tim acting as my translator. He explained to the vendors that if they pulled out they would need to pay me double the deposit. I let them know that it seemed like a great idea if they decided not to sell and I would be only too happy for them to pull out of the contract, with a little laughter among us. This part of the process, however, was critical and where estate agents really earn their money. With Tim I knew I was in safe hands.

After we had exchanged contracts, I returned to my humble abode delighted with the progress, still laughing at the events of the night before. This was meant to be the straightforward part.

6. Completion

Since my first trip I'd learnt how to reduce travel costs massively and secure the best deals available for hotels parking, flights, car hire and insurance. I saved literally hundreds per trip on the bookings so I decided to add to my workload and create a website with a mass online promotion to assist others.

For the next trip I decided to take Bargain Bill, my willing sidekick, with me to share the experience. I took my normal sequence of events when we landed in Faro: a short cut through customs with a little trick I learnt on the last visit, straight to my little trusted car gleaming in the morning sun ready and waiting. 'No need to upgrade, Bill,' I said as we walked over to the love of my life, well for that week at least.

Our first service stop was a great experience with fresh local salad, which was extremely large and a fraction of the cost of similar at home. So far I'd saved around 250 euros and trimmed down my time getting out of the airport by around thirty-five minutes. 'I mean business this time,' I boasted to Bill as were on our way.

Eventually we arrived at Vila Nova de Milfontes and headed straight for the hotel. For forty-five euros per night you can't expect perfection and total comfort in this part of the country, however, the rooms were comfortable and this was made better by the brilliant customer care that these amazing locals offer to their guests.

We did a tour around the town, visiting the little arty shops and local Chinese discount stores, which seemed to be springing up all over Portugal, where you can get some amazing bargains. This time under Bill's protective advice, I rented from the hotel a digital key safe to ensure my goods were protected including passport, ID and most importantly the cash to cover the 10% fees ready for the next day. Our lovely English-speaking receptionist took care of all our needs, all good so far so. What could possibly go wrong this time? But based on my previous experiences I remained focused but prepared for the unforeseen.

The day of reckoning. We got up early with plenty of time to travel from our hotel to Odemira and were looking forward to our 9 o'clock meeting over a nice continental breakfast with Tim, the vendors Riora and Dimitri and the local solicitor. It was all going far too well until I went to retrieve my documents from the safe, which is linked to a national computer network. I typed in the number three times and the safe went in to lock mode; there was some sort of technical error, which I assumed was down to the computer set up when we booked the safe out. After the beach fiasco I couldn't imagine any more setbacks, so I simply made my way to reception to capture the only English-speaking person to ask them to reset it.

I hurriedly arrived at reception but, unfortunately, no one was around. Eventually I found a pool maintenance guy going about his daily duties but discovered he spoke absolutely no English. After some fifteen minutes I was delighted to see the non-English-speaking receptionist.

To my dismay, I managed to work out that there was no easy way for this to be opened as it was controlled off site. The receptionist advised me in Portuguese that she couldn't help but a technical guy would come in an hour.

I managed to make it clear via Google Translate that I couldn't wait an hour and it needed to be rectified now, or the deposit for the house may be too late, and the hotel would receive a rather large bill. It wasn't clear at that time whether the technical guy was coming or not but eventually he arrived like a Portuguese knight in shining armour so I decided to call him António, meaning invaluable. I ushered him to the room to begin work almost pushing him up the stairs.

After quite some time trying to crack the code it repeatedly failed and I kept hearing, '*Nao, nao, mmmm, nao,*' with a little head scratching in between. This was not good. He was now extremely busy dealing with the technical department on his phone to try to bypass the security settings. I could tell he really believed that we had failed as his head repeatedly dropped with big sighs, but on the final attempt of cracking the code the lock released followed by a huge sigh of relief from all of us. Not for the first time it was time to go in to emergency mode.

I quickly gathered up my documents and cash and handed a rather large tip to a tired looking António, who thirty minutes earlier had been forced out of bed on his day off. Still looking dazed he suddenly came to life and was extremely happy with his bonus for the day. Eventually we met with Tim, Riora and Dimitri but luckily I had got the times wrong and we were able to grab a lovely Portuguese Delta coffee and a pain au chocolat before crossing the road to the solicitors, giving me a little time to chill out and get my mind straight again.

Dimitri and Riora were a couple of characters. Dimitri was destined to swim the seven seas although to Riora's enjoyment so far he has only managed to get lost for a day swimming the powerful swirls of the Mira River.

After we concluded our meeting we proceeded to the house. With no time to waste we quickly worked out material requirements for the next day. We visited the local hardware shop in my favourite town of Odemira, sneaking in another quick visit to the Chinese shop in order to reduce costs and the local snack bars for a coffee.

Back at the house I was busy applying sealant to the entire property, buzzing not because I'd just purchased my first property abroad but getting high on the fumes of the sealant. I was busy cleaning and generally getting the property into a reasonable condition for my next visit, but we weren't really prepared for this and as it got late, we decided to go to a local bar for a well-deserved ham and cheese toasty.

It resembled a 1960's lounge with a few elderly locals going about their daily chores and downing their locally produced port in two key stages before making their way to the next bar. There were only two small bars in the village but it seemed like a nice simple life.

After some Google translations, we ordered our food and drinks. As Bill and I sat there watching our sandwiches on the bar with a few flies hovering above, the man behind the counter picked them up and walked off down the street.

To our delight, he returned with tasty hot toasties. We tucked in and they were gone in twenty seconds; they were the best and weirdest toasties ever. We drank our ice-cold cokes and said, '*Adios* until the next time, *amigo*,' before trudging off up the road to check out the local supermarket.

We met a local builder, Rui, that night who had been introduced to us via the sellers and instantly I could see he was someone to be trusted, unlike quite a few builders I have had the misfortune of dealing with in the UK. He arrived on time with his translator, Tim, and we went through the list of items, which included shutters, double-glazed high security widows, fencing to the raised balcony and two locking gates as well as roof repairs. I left it to him to decide on the actual finishes, as that was part of the fun. When I received the quotes while back in the UK they were so reasonable I was amazed it could be done at those sorts of rates.

That night Bill and I had another amazing meal in Vila Nova de Milfontes before returning to the UK. I was extremely worn out by this time after trying to make as much progress as possible to get the property ready to sleep in. As soon as I got back it would be straight to the childminders to pick up the baby, feed her and do the washing-up, bringing me back to reality prior to returning to work in Clapham the next day. Gone were the empty roads running through scenic landscapes of Alentejo; hello to traffic horns honking away as I navigated my way through the constant road works in London. Welcome home, time to refocus once again on my day job.

7. The Return

It was a good feeling while undertaking my day job to know I had my little Portuguese bolthole after some difficult periods in my life. I was busy completing my various projects at work, but I knew my own project wouldn't be finished for some time. I still had white goods to source, bedding to purchase and loads of other considerations to create a real home from home. These days people are more focused on mobile phones than mobile homes as a priority, but if the children were expecting the home comforts of Wi-Fi, the closest that they were likely to get was a good old fashion game of Scrabble. I'd worry about that when they finally arrived, they may even embrace it, who knows?

For my next visit, I was fully intending to go alone but at the last minute my partner in crime Bargain Bill decided to come, but he preferred to stay on the coast in Vila Nova de Milfontes. It's only forty minutes away, how hard can that be, right? So I agreed it would be a great experience for both of us again.

On the day of arrival, I went through my usual routine: shortcut through customs followed by my express car from my preferred local supplier Goldcar, negotiate specialist VIP rate for insurance and free car upgrade, of course. Our first stop was at my favourite motorway service station where we grabbed an ice-cold coke and fresh sandwiches before reaching my village hideaway in the scenic valleys of Santiago. As we drove up it became clear that the villagers were coming out to look at the great

English explorers, and we went through our now well-rehearsed Portuguese greetings. Like the queen in her glass coach, Bill put it. I thought it was more like Del-boy and Rodney in their bright yellow three-wheel van.

I was blown away by the quality of my Portuguese builder's work. The quality was amazing; the metalwork was all custom-made to a standard I would never expect in the UK. I happily transferred the funds into Rui's bank account. *Muchio obrigado,* Rui.

We set to work straight away and I ran through item by item of works required. Bill was in charge of driving us forward with the actual hard graft by ordering loads of paint to carry out the substantial redecoration that was way above my original expectations, but still a worthwhile investment in time. Clearly this was not going to be the chilled-out lazy day experience that I was hoping for. We got stuck into things, preparing the walls and made list after list of materials for various work-streams, but we still found time for a number of coffee breaks to keep us both going where we sat up on the podium overlooking the animals grazing on the golden grass.

Once the list was created, we went to our favourite Chinese store in Odemira in search of materials. I managed to buy an amazing amount of goods for one hundred and twenty euros, which included everything with a few extra little gadgets kindly gifted from Bargain Bill. It was now quite late so we visited one of my original favourite Portuguese restaurants in De Milfontes for our three-course meal, which was a joy. Following a few diversions, I drove back another forty minutes and was really struggling at this point; it was going to be far harder than I first envisaged.

After four days of driving, touring, decorating and unexpected repairs, I calculated that I was doing around four hours per day driving, getting home around half ten every night after dropping Bill back to his hotel. Every time I got back to the village, I was greeted by the moonlight and bright shining stars to keep me awake. It was hard not to be passionately drawn to the natural beauty of the night sky.

After unloading my materials from the car, I started to go through my build-up of paper work prior to getting some well-earned sleep. I literally fell on the bed exhausted from the day's activities and even left the front door open, but after such a tough few days I really didn't care.

The mornings generally consisted of a quick bowl of cereal, freshly made Delta coffee, which was sampled on my little podium overlooking the lush green Alentejo countryside. I watched the goats and sheep wander down the steep banked hills with their little bells draped around their necks chiming out across the beautiful landscapes with the sounds of the chickens, dogs and church bells to complete the orchestra. The weather was stunning, not too hot but lovely and sunny, but for the locals it was like winter as they wandered around the village in their sweatshirts and woolly jumpers. For me it was t-shirts and shorts as summer had come early.

By the final night of an energy zapping week, I was absolutely exhausted. I was staying in Vila Nova de Milfontes for the last night in a lovely little family hotel by the name of Quinta Do Moinho De Vento, which was run by a friendly Portuguese couple who both spoke great English. It was such a warm atmosphere; I decided I would certainly return at some point. After sampling a few beers from their little bar, I retreated up the ceramic tiled staircase to my room. It was the best night's sleep in years due to utter exhaustion. I had a 4 a.m. wake up and a two-hour drive along dark country lanes.

I felt quite sad at this point as Bill and I said adios to the lovely lands of Portugal. I couldn't wait to return with the children; there would be no hard graft. *Até a próxima vez.*

At the airport, I had a brilliant idea to start documenting my travels on my iPhone SE to share the wonders of the real Portugal with the world; the one that tourists rarely see while in the tourist areas. I wanted to show a more refined experience complete with fine wines and the best local produce, to mention just a few delights. I started straight away while the thoughts were fresh in my mind, and at this point I discovered how hard it would be as I could barely see the tiny screen and time after time the auto text would correct my spellings. This would become normal practice throughout my experience, constantly updating my blog while flying high at 40,000 feet. Eventually the Money Saving Tree blog was born, which in turn funded much of my travels as well as a few optional extras for my little casa in the sun.

I still, however, never considered the size of the project, including working around various social media changes, which were affecting the online marketing gurus. I realised that my blog would fail to earn any sort of profit, so I needed to seek out other ideas. The only real option was an ambitious plan to ditch my blog and write possibly the first book in the world using an I Phone SE. I constantly put my experiences and thoughts together as holidaymakers looked on in amazement at this crazy person typing away like his life depended on it from the salt pans of Faro to the shores of the UK.

8. Children's Time

I felt a little stressed after the previous night, which started with an Olly Murs concert at the O2 arena on the Greenwich peninsula for my demanding son followed by a high speed run through the streets of Greenwich and Charlton after boarding the wrong bus back to my car. Clearly this was not the best start to the following day.

After arriving home around midnight, I managed to at least lay my weary head down for a few hours but was kept awake pre-planning the onward journey. It would be the first time abroad with my children, which for me was a huge moment and hopefully special for them as well.

When we arrived at the little casa, we walked through the ornate front entrance door in anticipation. I was surprised by the smell of stale air and condensation. My children rushed through the door eager to stake a claim on their room with Elliott first claiming the large sofa bed in the lounge and Ruby claiming the bunk beds prior to searching through the desk drawers for pencils and paper, which were awaiting her craft skills.

I searched in vain to seek out any uninvited little guests that may have been attracted to the empty property, but all I found were a few tiny spiders and my friendly lizard residing in the courtyard lapping up the glorious sunshine.

Once the children had explored their surroundings, we headed out to explore. We drove down the isolated country roads, past a few wild, stray cats when Elliott casually asked, 'Dad, can stray wild cats have collars on?'

'Yes son,' I replied. 'They all go to a little cat store in the mountains owned by Moggy the store keeper.' At that point he realised his teenage comment and we all laughed as we drove through the rich landscape while I pointed out various interesting landmarks such as the hilltop flower mills.

Arriving at the deserted beaches on the west coast, we headed straight out to the water's edge and had so much fun playing ball games and scoffing down our picnic lunches. We explored the caves and rock pools then visited the aptly named Oásis restaurant, close to the brilliantly unspoilt Furnas Beach. As we walked in Ruby discovered an abundance of freshly caught crabs and lobsters all scurrying around in the tank unaware of their fate and she refused to walk past the tank.

The week was a very special experience and the people in the village loved Ruby; they considered her cheeky and loved her style of dress, which was typical of most eight-year-old girls in the UK. The shopkeepers couldn't wait to bring all the ladies in the village to see her and give her little playful squeezes. She was treated like a princess and she loved the attention. Although slightly shy, she managed to learn a little Portuguese to impress the locals and really seemed to embrace the experience.

Elliott was clearly enjoying himself but I wondered if as a typical teenager he might struggle in the sun-lavished lands on future trips due to a lack of technology, which I was keen to keep him away from in order to experience the simple life.

During this visit we created a lovely home from home, picking up loads of little comfort goods on our travels, slowly providing character to match the location deep in the valleys of Santiago.

This was meant to be the week where I was budgeting, but unfortunately it didn't quite work that way as we frequented just about every beach restaurant and snack bar in all the towns we visited. I also spent vast sums on Ruby's craft items and decorations for her planned sculpture in my little bathroom. We didn't explore as much as we would've liked due to the various matters I needed to attend to. We did quickly meet Tim, our brilliant estate agent at the Remax offices in Milfontes, and consumed generous amounts of ice cream from Mabi, the best ice cream parlour and coffee bar in this part of Portugal.

In no time at all the entire experience seemed to be over and I really wished I'd booked some additional time. I even considered accidentally missing the flight home in order to extend our stay.

It was a great experience having my children at my side through this holiday and I was amazed at my new language skills picked up during this latest trip. I discovered loads of amazing words from urban street slang for things such as the old classic 'sik' as well as loads of others including bait – suspicious; bare – cost loads; banning – great time; and creps – trainers. Apparently my little hire car was not actually 'so fly', which I assumed meant cool, and there was me thinking I was with it bruv, perhaps not! It was an enlightening experience to say the least.

9. Week of Reckoning

After a really fun time going through the entire process of buying, organising works using my brilliant local builder Rui, touring the local areas with my sidekick Bargain Bill and then with my kiddies who I got to spend quality time with, it was time for my partner and youngest child to attend. This would be the ultimate test, as Samantha had never really showed the same level of enthusiasm that I had for the property. How would she adapt to such a simple alternative lifestyle deep in the valleys?

With this in mind, I chose to start with a week in the Algarve. On the day we arrived, the summer kicked in with sizzling temperatures, which was good for relaxing Samantha's mind prior to turning up at our little house in the isolated village of Santiago. I hoped that she would embrace the stunningly simple way of life in the beautiful countryside.

During May there had been quite a lot of rainfall. This was good news as there had been no rain at all in the entire time I'd gone through the house buying process. The locals were a little worried as they rely on the rain to harvest the water, which runs through the concrete channels cut through the hills and mountains to the reservoirs. If it's too hot, the water runs down the channels and as it touches the scorching concrete it evaporates, which is quite bad for the water retention and in turn a real worry for the environment.

It really was a joy to see the dry rivers transformed into crystal clear and fast flowing rivers bristling with life.

We stayed just outside Albufeira in the Alfagar apartments, a brilliant little holiday village close to Olhos de Agua, which was previously a sleepy little fishing village. The area has started to bring in increased tourism but still with the added bonus of great local prices where you could pick up a four-course meal for the amazing price of only eight euros, far below the tourist rates you pay in other areas.

At the hotel, we were instantly recognised due to two previous visits over the years. We were pleasantly surprised at how nice the apartment was. It was a very busy week, generally starting in the gym followed by a four-mile walk to the shops, then pool and then more food, arriving home around 9.30 every night. We visited all the local places including the lovely Vilamora and the old town and it was clear that it was going to be hard to beat this.

On the day we checked out of the hotel, we took the transfer back to the airport then picked up the usual car from Goldcar before setting off on our journey just north of the Algarve, stopping off at my regular haunts. This time things seemed different; I was almost able to understand the language and signage as well as dropping a few Portuguese words into my sentences.

Driving up country to my sleepy village, it felt like the place was coming alive. There was a noticeable increase in animals appearing from all corners of the green valley, and fast flowing water had replaced the dry rivers. The locals were tending their fields with big smiles on their faces in the heat of the midday sun, which was reaching eighty-four degrees. These guys deserved a medal; it's not easy but they generally remain happy and content with life, which is a lesson to learn for us all.

I started to wonder if my grapevines had survived the hot weather and if Rui had locked the door upon completing his works. Are my six-inch grasshoppers still taking residency in my featured garden bush and, the most important thing, what will Amelia (age two and three quarters) make of this? As we got closer it was impossible not to have any negative thoughts especially since Amelia's latest talk is about monsters, bears, wild cats (without collars) and wild animals! Hopefully we could settle for a casual stroll to the village through the flock of sheep grazing on the grass.

We drove up the dusty dirt track to the village and could hear the church bells in the distance. When we arrived at our little Portuguese casa we were delighted to be welcomed to the village by local families eager to find out more about us.

Samantha seemed quite apprehensive as we entered the house while Amelia asked, 'Daddy, can we go back to Portugal? I don't like it here it smells.' This relieved the tension and I explained to Amelia that the lovely smell is the honest smell of a little casa in the village of Santiago, which all the houses had and I assured her that once the air started to flow the smell would disappear. Try explaining that to a toddler. All appeared to be fine so there was no need for me to trigger my emergency action plan of a quick tent purchase from the Chinese shop and a last minute booking to one of the amazing camp sites in Milfontes. Instead we settled for an early night and a nice cup of cocoa sitting overlooking the lovely fields that surround the village with just the sounds of the animals in the background.

10. Walk Time

We went for a walk through the village the next morning, stopping to talk to every local. They were blown away by Amelia's cheeky smile and newly found Portuguese language skills due to the time she'd spent listening to dad's CD in the back of his UK car. It's a shame dad's memory isn't as good as Amelia's.

The locals were gathering by an attractive rustic water well to pick up their daily water supply, and they tried to teach us how to scoop up the water in the tin bucket. I'd never considered how such a basic thing could be so hard and I decided it was time to show off my skills. I repeatedly struggled to get the tiniest drop of water in the old tin bucket attached to the long thing rope. I never imagined how such a basic action could take so much practice and I constantly only manged to float the bucket on top of the water in the bottom of the well.

After about fifteen minutes of trying, with Amelia getting rather frustrated and the locals laughing, it was obvious that I was better off being a surveyor than a humble water gatherer and I decided to swear allegiance to my village shop owner and buy my water pre-bottled straight off the shelf.

We walked further into the village past loads of little whitewashed homes decorated with ornate ceramic tiles and eventually we came across a lovely lady who was extremely eager to talk to Amelia. Amelia loved this as she received a little squeeze or two, loads of cuddles and even more smiles and it was clear how much the locals love their children. We were invited into the house to meet the lady's husband, and she couldn't wait to show off the new little English girl to her family. She was also eager to show me photos of her own granddaughter who was the same age but lived in Spain due to the lack of opportunities for the local people which was a shame, but clearly she was so proud.

After twenty minutes or so we were back on the little dirt track via the hill, which we named name Columbus Hill due to the historical information I had previously uncovered on my journey. Bells were tinkling in the background and we came to a derelict church in the middle of a field, which was unexpected. I wondered if this could possibly be the real birthplace of Christopher Columbus and intended to do a little more research on the subject later, but this was Amelia's moment.

We came across an elderly farmer who was busy lugging barrow after barrow of feed up the hill steep cone shaped hill so we gave him a little wave and I helped him drag the barrow up the last section, much to his appreciation and he repeatedly shook my hand.

Eventually we got to the top of the hill and gazed out over the stunning landscape. There was and an abundance of olive, cork, eucalyptus and fruit trees stretching out into the distance, which continued through to the stunning mountains in the background. We stood there just staring, humbled by the beautiful landscape.

Suddenly Amelia became hysterical and when I looked down I saw that we were standing in a rather large ants nest. Huge ants were running over our feet so I pulled Amelia away, frantically brushing them off her while doing a strange type of Portuguese tap dance specially created for getting ants out of your open front sandals, much to the enjoyment of the farmer who was laughing and gave me a little clap. That's when it occurred to me that I knew absolutely nothing about living in the countryside other than the fact that there were animals and insects. Next time I'll come with my waking shoes and be prepared for the task ahead.

We walked back down the little dirt track towards the village and I explained to Amelia that ants are fun, and the big ants the size of her toe nails are actually her friends so there was no need to be scared. She burst into a big smile, gave me a huge cuddle and whispered, 'I love you, Daddy,' as we navigated our way down the dry dusty track.

We passed Amelia's favourite lady's house and she came out and gave her another little squeeze, and proudly showed me more photos of her lovely family. After a few minutes I looked round to discover Amelia had taken me at my word and picked up the biggest ant I'd ever seen. She was delighted to show her new friend that she wasn't scared anymore as she clutched the ant in her fingers; the poor thing was moving wildly from side to side trying to escape her embrace. I managed to talk her into letting go so that he could go home to his family for dinner with the baby ants and she reluctantly agreed to let it return to nature.

Walking back through the village, there were loads of people and an energetic atmosphere. According to a poster on the local noticeboard, it was festival weekend. We worked out that that the event was especially for family members to reunite with their family and friends in the village for which they travelled from all around the world.

It sounded like a good opportunity to meet the locals and find out more about both the village and its lovely people.

Later that day we noticed a stage being set up at the local social club, so we ventured in to see if we could use the facilities. Instantly we were welcomed with big smiles from the locals, and we even discovered a Wi-Fi code, which may not have been the best thing.

We set up our mobiles and communicated with the staff using Google Translate, and we were introduced to a friendly young guy called Giovani. Fortunately for us he spoke perfect English and we were given the run down on the festival that was happening the next day.

He told us about the annual event and we discovered that his dad, Mr Camisa, was supplying the best black pig money could buy and cooking it on a traditional spit roast, which was also supplied buy him. Music would played on the newly erected stage that was also built and supplied by him. Giovani further explained that it was only twelve euros for all you could eat and drink, and they would be really pleased if we could join them. We gladly accepted and after a few drinks in the bar and a game of chase Amelia around the club game, we made our way back to our little casa looking forward to the up and coming experience.

11. Festival Fun

We woke up to the funky cockerels bellowing out at full volume on the day of the festival. There wasn't a huge amount of time left so we decided to take things a little easy by spending some time in the village, popping into the local towns to visit a few coffee bars, patisseries, ice cream parlours and another Chinese shop or two. It was a sunny day and as we arrived back at the village we could hear the general excitement and preparation for the festival.

After a day of relaxation, we walked to the local social club and were happy to be greeted by our new friend Giovani. Despite rushing around organising things, he still took the time to explain to us how to join in the fun. This was so typical of the people in this area of Portugal.

In the main hall, there were rows and rows of benches and tables overflowing with food, and the wine was served in traditional Portuguese jugs. Literally hundreds of people were all drinking, singing, laughing and hugging each other. Amelia was happily running up and down between the tables weaving in and out of the locals standing in her way while traditional folk music was delightfully performed in the background.

The stage was in the main area with more rows of tables and the locals were dancing to the live music. Amelia couldn't wait to show the entire village her dancing skills and, much to my amazement, she was very much in time with the music, not bad for a two year old. It was a lovely experience so far and the amazing smell of the pork being roasted over the flaming charcoal grill made me hungrier by the minute, so hungry I could eat a pig.

We helped ourselves to beer after beer from the tap and were blown away by the smell of what is known to be the best quality black pork in Portugal, turning constantly and basted with the finest olive oil and fresh herbs sourced from the chef's own garden. The herbs and oil were applied with a bunch of rosemary tied together to create the basting brush. The juices soaked into the meat gave it the most incredible taste, far superior to any meat I've ever had anywhere else in the world, and was complemented with traditional locally baked sweet Alentejo bread served up in dishes with little pots of olive oil and balsamic vinegar.

Amelia made friends with another little girl in the village, who was three with a lovely smile and the cutest curls. They were then inseparable holding hands as they played throughout the night although Amelia was quite concerned that the little girl wasn't talking. I tried to explain that we speak a different language, but she was more interested in running around with her new friend.

Unfortunately Samantha left slightly early as she was feeling a little poorly, so Amelia and I stayed. Later she dragged me across the road to her favourite play park where I was forced to play her favourite monster game while a pack of wild cats looked on bemused.

By the time we got back to the party, it had gone up a gear and we chatted to Giovani. He told us that he comes back for the summer but also works as a chef in various restaurants around Europe, gradually introducing the restaurants to his traditional Portuguese cooking styles. Judging by the amazing taste of black pig and his secret family recipe that has been passed down through the generations he would be a real benefit to any restaurant.

As we talked, Giovani told us of his plans. To keep his dad's restaurant supply business going, he intends to offer free meals charging only fees to cover the costs of the food as a non-profit venture and he came across an idea of a pop-up restaurant. He invited us all to his place the next day to try out his idea. As we left, Amelia said, '*Adios amigo*,' and we departed to our little casa while the music intensified across the village, which eventually finished in the early hours of the morning shortly after the almost mystical music shut down. What an amazing night I thought as I shut my eyes falling in to an exceptionally deep sleep.

12. Pop-up Restaurant Experience

I've visited a number of restaurants in my time, which is well highlighted by the fact I have ended up in London's top 1% on TripAdvisor, and I was very much looking forward to attending my first pop-up kitchen experience with Giovani and Mr Camisa. Unfortunately both Amelia and Samantha were feeling under the weather. We decided to try a little shopping, but this was quite a major chore as we had a poorly little girl who'd manged to catch a virus from her cousins and she struggled through the day. We knew that she would need some medicine and an early night to try to get her better for the flight in a few days' time so I was forced to go it alone. Tough life but someone has to do it I thought as I got mentally prepared.

When we got back to the village, we walked down to the social club where we found Giovani eager to show off the kitchen skills that had been passed down through the generations of the Camisa family. I gave Amelia and Samantha a quick peck on their sun-bronzed cheeks and promised to be home soon, well not quite a 100% promise and maybe not even 50%, but I jumped in the car and off we went to talk business, well talk at least. I had no idea of the delightful offerings that were yet to come.

As we drove up to the edge of the village, two stunning properties came into sight both painted in classic sunshine yellow and white. We headed up the drive to the grounds, passing the little dog that was at the gate keeping guard. He was clearly excited at our arrival judging by the speed that his tail wagged and he came dashing over to see us as we walked through the large compound gates.

We walked through a landscaped garden with lush thick green grass, natural rock cladding, driftwood skilfully placed and reclaimed rope from the local beaches built up over many years. It was like being to an isolated island in the middle of the deep blue sea, just without the sea or the deadly crocodiles.

All the family were there to greet me and I was made to feel really welcome. This was a million miles away from my expectation when I purchased my property in the village. Every item on show in the garden had a different story to tell and as the food was slowly grilled to perfection in the background, we went through a lesson in the production of cork then a wine tasting workshop and that was all before the food was even served.

The premium quality Alentejo wine was poured and much to my delight I was taught some wine tasting skills. As I drank the first glass of vino tinto, the sun was scorching the top of the tree-lined hills and I realised how lucky was to have found such a wonderfully amazing place.

The first course was a combination of fresh local goats' cheese, which simply melted in the mouth, alongside a gorgeous selection of the finest Parma ham matured and cured to perfection. This was served with chouriço, a Portuguese sausage, neatly sliced along with the local freshly baked sweet Portuguese bread.

After a few minutes, more plates came out. They were piled up with the most amazing selection of fresh salad all sprinkled with herbs and dressed with local fruit, including the gorgeous oranges straight from their kitchen garden. We tucked in to this splendid feast, overlooking the hills at the entrance to the village and listening to the goats, sheep, chickens and other habitants while the black pork sizzled on the BBQ as the juice touched the red hot charcoal.

Finally as we embraced the main course, Giovani enthusiastically prepared gin & tonics, incorporating a combination of spices to give the most incredible sweet smell. Wow, it packed a punch or two.

The sun started to set beyond the distant hills and at that point I said adios to the family and thanked them for their kindness. My young chef friend and I then headed to the lake hidden down a little isolated dirt track five minutes from the village in order to experience pure relaxation.

As we got closer I could see the lake teaming with life surrounded by the long sun-baked grass. There were loads of traditional cork and eucalyptus trees in the middle of the unspoilt countryside and various deserted natural stone buildings with no one to be seen as the sun dropped behind the distant Alentejo hills. What a fitting way to end the experience I thought as the sun started to quickly set. We decided to make our way back to the village ready for me to catch some well-earned sleep, albeit slightly later than anticipated but after my over indulgence it didn't take long for me to drop back in to the theatre of dreams on my little soft Chinese sourced pillow.

13. Final Discovery Day

On the last day, I woke at sunrise to the sound of swallows flying in and out of my porch, causing the traditional brass doorbell to ring out like wind chimes in a gentle breeze. As I stood ready to enjoy my last day, I realised it was my destiny to catch this dreaded virus and my legs virtually gave way.

So we decided to stay local and explore the village, hoping to find some hidden treasures, which we may have previously overlooked. We headed to the other side of the village and discovered a tiny road leading to an isolated group of houses with traditional whitewashed walls banded with the equally typical blue and orange colour schemes consistent throughout the Alentejo region. This area of the village had a large number of derelict properties complete with collapsing roofs, corrugated rusty metal forming a cover over the rotted timber doors and all in need of a loving restoration project to bring the area back to life.

It occurred to me that people pass away and leave properties for their loved ones, who have long left the village in the search of a better life. The properties fall into disrepair, starting a domino effect. Unless this trend is reversed, the entire area will remain stagnant and it would take something a little special to reverse this natural migration progress so maybe there will be some winners after the Brexit fiasco.

I figured that in the current condition the plots could be purchased at rates in the region of 13,000 euros. Allowing a relatively small development figure of 22,000 euros per unit, you could have a reasonable holiday rental catering for ramblers, bikers and fishing parties for a budget of 35,000 euros. Local labour could be used for the project to help local businesses start to flourish again, which hopefully would encourage more locals back to the village in the long term.

After around an hour, the sun rays were shining down intensely on my receding hairline, which was now a delightful tomato colour. I was struggling to stand as I felt my temperature rising.

I walked back to my little casa and said my *obrigados* to the village people as they bid me farewell until my return. I was happy that I didn't need to pack any clothes, just my passport, flight tickets and, oh yes, better not forget Amelia and Samantha. There was still a full day of cleaning including the kitchen and bathroom as well as mopping every floor in the property before leaving. Perhaps it wasn't quite as easy as I'd first thought, but it had certainly been a rewarding and life-changing experience on this latest journey of discovery.

I did wonder if it would have been easier to acquire a small apartment in the English-speaking region of Albufeira, complete with the anti-social behaviour that goes hand in hand with the traditional English binge drinking culture. Was I correct in opting for the Alentejo farmland region with wild growing fruit, fresh produce and some of the finest wines in Europe? I will let others decide.

14. Operation Stealth

It was now the middle of summer and I was taking my oldest two children back to the village. This time I planned things a couple of days prior to flying.

The weather was perfect and after short stop for cold drinks and ice creams, we headed straight to the Alfagar hotel for a day at the pool. As we weren't residents of the hotel, I briefed the children to try to blend in as much as possible; however, I failed to consider their milky white skin and my youngest one's inquisitive nature.

As we arrived we unpacked some supplies such as sun cream. A big stern looking woman was speaking loudly into her mobile phone and monitoring our every move. Ruby asked question after question regarding our mission. I was actually quite nervous but didn't want to spoil their day by not going so we popped into the village to purchase supplies from the shop including a large floaty in an attempt to justify our pool day by spending our cash.

We went to the poolside restaurant and the stern looking woman reappeared. She watched us extremely closely as I ordered our food and drink, and I mentioned to the waiter how well he looked and how it was far busier than when I was there the previous two times this year. He assumed that we had just arrived, went over to Mrs Stern and showed her my receipt and I knew that we could now enjoy a free day by the pool.

It was a lovely day and we went to various pools in the complex including the leisure pool with slides and water jets, and then on to the more secluded pool on top of the sandstone cliff edge, overlooking the stunningly scenic Algarve coast.

After loads of fun we decided a final crack at the leisure pool was needed. As we headed down to the play area I noticed that all the guests we wearing bright red wristbands; that's when I realised my cunning plan was flawed. An angry Mrs Stern and the desk manager were marching towards us at great speed, so I ordered the kids to quickly pack up the supplies and decant to our rescue vehicle parked at the emergency evacuation point (*EVP*). We made it just in time and drove off to explore the delights of the local McDonald's, which we were shocked and surprised to discover didn't serve milkshakes.

While there, we strolled to the large shopping area to pick up a BBQ and a new booster seat for Ruby. The next challenge was getting it all in the hire car but we eventually after some effort managed it and were on our way to Vale de Santiago, although it would have been better without a BBQ leg out of the window.

As we arrived, we waved as usual to the bench dwelling locals who sit in the sun talking and laughing their way through the day. It was so nice to see such a simple life and it instantly made us feel welcomed and relaxed.

Ruby was first through the door to check her bedroom hadn't been disturbed, and much to her delight her desk was still there, but she was oblivious to the 600 euros spent on damp proofing the wall. We went into the garden and discovered hundreds of bunches of grapes dangling from the vines producing an abundance of red and green fruit draping down from the rich green vines.

From the podium area, we saw horses casually wandering around and grazing on the straw-like grass. Not too far away there was a traditional horse drawn carriage with supplies piled high ready for the family's travels. The parents were making craft items while the children played happily around the fruit trees, occasionally reaching up to harvest the sweet offerings. It was hard not to be a little jealous of their uncomplicated life, but in reality they were forced to remain on the road day after day in the intense heat searching for food. That night I wondered what would happen when the free growing fruit had all dropped from the trees so I decided to get up early and deliver my grapes to them to help them on their travels.

15. Next Day Arrives

The next day I got up at 7.15, which was evident by the church bells going off for the second time in that hour. Then I remembered the gypsy family and went to check if they were still there, but they were nowhere to be seen. I was a little disappointed but at the same time felt happy that they were back on their horse and cart resuming their travels.

We went to Vila Nova de Milfontes and were amazed by the change from a little sleepy arty town to a bustling seaside town packed solid with locals and a few Dutch and Germans along with various New Age travelling types. Everyone was eager to experience the lovely atmosphere that the town had to offer with a large castle, streets and streets of brilliant restaurants, snack bars and the most amazing ice cream bar by the name on Mabi's, which was a big hit with my happy children.

A little tired from the travelling, we headed down to the beach. Most of the locals appeared to model themselves on a Portuguese version of David Beckham, their footballing genius in the form of Ronaldo, immaculate in appearance and constantly smiling and laughing while showing off their barefoot footballing skills. I couldn't wait to spread my towel out and lay down while Elliott played with his sister. As soon as we got the towels from the bag, he put his cap over his head and fell asleep. That left me to play with Ruby, no rest for the wicked!

We strolled over the soft sand in the brilliant midday sun to the laurel green water at the mouth of the

Mira River. It was cascading across the sands leaving behind a white water foam, sinking gently into the sand before disappearing from sight while the waves withdrew out to sea to join the powerful swells of the Atlantic.

The kids sneaked up behind me, and floored me with an inflatable penguin. As I stood I felt myself go backwards as a flying kick headed towards me by little legs and I was submerged in the cold water, which brought me back to life quite quickly. No longer was it a river of poetic wonders; it was a cold ice block, but after a few minutes it was my time to lay down and relax. After a little while we went up past the castle to the local Paparoca for something to eat.

I intended to leave early but by the time we had been served and wandered around the town once again, the sun had disappeared although we did have the moonlight shining down to guide us home at around midnight.

16. Mystical Sintra Experience

I was up early once again and straight into my usual routine. I switched on my super cool coffee machine, and disappeared up to my podium to chill out during sunrise watching the swallows fly around. A little head appeared at almost the same time each day.

'Daddy, where we going today?'

'Today, my darling, I've a wonderful experience for you. We're exploring Lisboa, or Lisbon to you, to take in the sights and the culture.'

'Oh great, Dad. Can I take shaggy?'

Shaggy is fluffy, about six inches tall and considered a must-have sleeping companion along with Mr Monkey and her amazing dream catcher, but I refused that request as the car was full. Next predictable question was what's for breakfast.

After a little chaotic packing, we set off on our road trip. We left the dirt and gravel tracks of the Alentejo for the motorways all the way through to Lisbon stopping off along the way at one or two service stations.

Before crossing the Portuguese version of the golden gate bridge into the centre of Lisbon, we headed up through the local suburb in search of a stunningly attractive piece of architecture in the form of Jesus Christ, reaching out high above the sensational fast flowing Tagus River. It runs all the way from the Iberian Peninsula to Spain until it spills out with a huge force joining the powerful swells of the Atlantic Ocean, but not before it passes below the impressive 25 de Abril Bridge. According to a clever looking elderly gent, it was named to commemorate the Carnation Revolution and has stood proud since 1974.

After a few missed turnings with my trusted Google friend, coupled with a few skirmishes with the local parking patrols in Almada, we managed to navigate our way to the Sanctuary of Christ the King. We were instantly blown away by the stunning design reaching up some 260ft with arms stretched out from its humble perch perfectly positioned to keep watch over the magnificent city of Lisbon watching the armada ships come and go to lands afar.

We managed to grab a few ice creams prior to entering the monument, which opened at 10 a.m., so we were one of the first groups of tourists to arrive looking for divine inspiration. We parted with our funds and took the lift to the top of the monument; it was impossible not to be humbled by both the view and the hard work put in to creating the amazing structure.

After doing a few loops around the top of the structure in the scorching sunshine admiring the craftsmanship, we spent a little time looking for perfect photo opportunities. Then we visited the gift shop and accidently pulled the head off a statue of Mary, which was quickly placed on the back of the shelf while no one was looking. We came across a very stern faced shop assistant taking the cash barely able to break a smile. I wondered if she'd seen our mishap as she took our hard-earned euros. The lack of smile surprised me as she was literally working directly below the feet of Jesus, so instead of divine inspiration we ended up with a couple of overpriced gifts although we did take some amazing photos. It was worth the experience just for the stunning views; we all felt blessed.

Before we left, Ruby wanted to put her money in to turn on the candle light on a little gadget within the church quarter. I informed her that she'd get a free magical wish to last a lifetime and the good luck that went with it. Perhaps I went a bit overboard as she then had another go, then another and eventually stopped at seven. At least we had a candle light to show for it; with regard to the magical wish and the lifetime of luck, we will see.

As we left, we were amazed by the amount of people entering the magnificent structure. One man explained that he was making a pilgrimage all the way from China to see it; I desperately hope he found what he was searching for, but if not they served some lovely coffee in the restaurant.

'Next stop Sintra, kids,' I shouted as we all jumped into our neat little hire car. We had survived so far but now the real test of my driving ability would be tested as crossed over the bridge and straight through the heart of Lisbon.

We weaved our way through the streets eager to arrive at our second and most prized destination. When we finally got to the motorway, we were delighted by the lack of traffic. At the V charge barrier, an alarm bell rang along with flashing red lights. I looked around to seek assistance but couldn't see anyone, so attempted to reverse; by now fifty or so cars were behind me sounding their horns. I had no choice but to continue, a little nervous about the possibility of a huge fine, but luckily for me it was confirmed that no charges had been made at the end of the holiday.

About half an hour later we finally made it to our destination in one of the most beautiful towns I had ever come across.

'*Olá, Sintra,*' Ruby shouted.

The town was an incredible mix of stunning architecture, shops and thousands of happy locals and tourists. Some were walking in the glorious golden sunshine while others were sitting around eating and drinking. This buzzy little town in the foothills of Sintra Mountain was used by the royal family for sanctuary. Its rich green forest and pastel coloured villas and mansions were perched gracefully high up in the mountainside with Pena Palace taking centre stage. It was an impressive sight with its brightly coloured construction topped off with a huge domed roof providing a mystical and romantic feeling. The palace would have to wait, though, as we headed towards the equally impressive Quinta da Regaleira, with Initiation Well dug out and carved deep into the mountain.

17. Quinta da Regaleira Time

As we drove up the steep mountain roads, I decided to try to spin around and look for a back way due to the high volume of traffic. Luckily there was one, but not before I had a slight disagreement with both Siri and Google Maps who both thought it would be more convenient to take me six miles away to a little back street housing estate. Eventually we got back on track after a nice man sitting in his car helped us, so off we went but this time we took the back route up the mountain.

We arrived at what we thought was our destination and as we parked and eagerly burst our way through the front entrance doors in our shorts and t-shirts, we were met by a bemused concierge, smiling from ear to ear. As he approached I realised we had the wrong building; we were standing in one of the most lavish hotels I'd ever seen. He kindly directed us further up the mountain road where we saw a large group of people; we had arrived at our mystical metropolis deep in the rich green and rocky forest.

The Initiation Well consisted of the finest sandstone rocks propped up with attractive ornate pillars finished off with crafted corbeling stones as it descended twenty-seven metres into the mountainside. As we climbed down the spiral staircase we were left in awe at the network of tunnels cut into the mountain.

We ventured deeper into the tunnels and the kids were both excited and nervous, but they fully embraced this magical experience along with the constant stream of excitable tourists with their voices echoing through the sandstone chambers and caverns below.

In one of the chambers, we discovered a pool of clear spring water and as soon as Ruby clapped eyes on it she scooped the water in slow motion, throwing it towards me. It missed me and landed on an unfortunate German man who literally froze prior to turning around, luckily this gave us a little time to make our escape down the dark tunnels and back out into the mystical enchanted woodlands arriving back into daylight, slightly embarrassed and red faced but with big smirks on the children's faces.

To our delight, we saw some stepping stones perched in the green lagoon complete with a stunning waterfall cascading over the natural rock face. It was like being transported back in time into a little tranquil fantasy world where nothing really mattered.

Further into the forest, there were more hidden little delights: grottos leading from the amazing tunnel complex, an aquarium cut into the rock with glass inserts to hold in the magical blessed water, a portal of the guardian's twin towers, a magnificent crafted chapel and the impressive ornate main house with beautiful landscaped gardens. The kids absolutely loved their adventure in the mystic tranquil world and I only lost them once but managed to find them when it was lunchtime, so not bad going.

It really was a magical experience and it was great to visit the café in the gardens of this stately home, which surprisingly offered great value for money. Before we departed we visited the main house to admire both the ornate architecture and fine art paintings that hung in every room on every wall while Ruby played art critic prior to getting bored.

Once again we failed to return to the village before pure darkness. In the back of the car, little eyes were fast asleep and as Ruby snored, Elliott and I talked about the amazing day, where he looked at me and thanked me for such an amazing experience.

On the flight back to the UK, we shared our memories of this special holiday experience with the hotel and water park taking centre stage for the kids, while I talked adoringly about our sub-ground adventures. Then I dropped them off at their mum's so we could all return to normality in our busy lives, until my next trip.

18. September Days

My airport days were now a little too routine; they involved getting up at 2.15 a.m., jumping on an early flight to land in Faro at 9 a.m. This time, however, a slightly more senior gent was sitting next to me anxiously awaiting the emergence of his wife who had been wheeled down to the aircraft some twenty minutes prior to his arrival. Unfortunately for this poor chap she seemed to have disappeared in the airport leaving him franticly pacing up and down the cockpit. I tried to reassure him by saying that she had possibly been taken to the VIP lounge and been busy drinking champagne and eating caviar; I explained she would turn up but by that point even I was feeling nervous. Eventually she turned up with loads of other passengers on a missing minibus and we were able to get sky bound. The delighted staff and passengers all gave an extremely loud cheer.

On landing, I walked straight through customs, giving my usual *bom dia* greeting to the friendly airport customs staff. The airport was eerily empty for that time of year.

Hitting the road once again with my trusted Goldcar rental, I made my way straight to Ikea with my family club card in search of goods, free coffee and a good old fashion chill out for a bit. Then I drove to Albufeira where I enjoyed a quick drink at the marina while watching the yachts as they arrived and moored up in the calm still water.

Once satisfied and mentally recharged, I picked up the main west coast road, which runs parallel with the Atlantic Ocean until I came across a little historic market town by the name of Aljezu. It came complete with a castle up on the steep hill keeping watch over a town packed with lovely bars, cafés and a fresh fish, fruit and veg market.

I parked and walked over the bridge, which spanned across what should have been a fast flowing river bristling with life. But, to my dismay, the water had been replaced in part by plants and seedlings taking root due to the drought, which really made me realise how important it is to protect the environment.

Before getting back on the road, I could see some cows and bulls grazing in the golden fields near my car. I couldn't resist, so I wandered over being careful to approach slowly from the side and gave the cows and bulls a pat on the side of their powerful necks. It was great until the largest bull in the field threw his head back with his horns rising upwards and gave a large grunt, sending shockwaves across the fields. I took this as my hint to leave and walked at a slightly more hurried pace from the herd, eventually running like a scared little kitten, while they continued munching on their lunch in the midday sun. *Adios amigos.*

After buying lunch and an abundance of tools and supplies in Odemira, followed by a detour for a drink at my favoured Furnas Beach bar, I headed to Cercal for some more local food supplies and then to my brilliant little village. I was delighted to see that the swallows had returned weaving their way around various inflight obstacles in the slightly dark blue skies, leaving me instantly relaxed.

By this time it was 6.30 p.m. and I was quite tired so I decided to unpack and go and say *Olá* to Celeste in her local convenience store. There was no sign of Alonso sitting in his usual position on the bench outside. I had become accustomed to him always greeting me; obviously, I'd missed him for the day. After greetings and supplies, I decided to retire to bed early.

Today was going to be a beach day, lying around in the sun watching the waves come and go with the sound of the sea birds in the background. But my quick gardening venture to harvest the grapes would not be simple. As soon as I opened the door my green grape vines were being dive bombed from all directions by hornet wasps, and I knew it would be a considerably time consuming task. Instead of harvesting them and giving them to the local villagers, I was forced to use a little cockroach spray to try to keep the wasps away while quickly trimming back the vines. With this new unforeseen risk, I cut back all vines rather than attempt to manage the growth over the year. Little by little I successfully cut back the lower vines constantly fighting off the hornets with a bright pink table tennis bat like a true English warrior as they flew at me from all directions.

Eventually all the vines were cut and on the floor of my tiled courtyard. I began to gather the spoils and bagged them up with a sense of achievement but this didn't last long. Out of the vines marched one extremely large and angry centipede, making its way right towards me stamping his many legs as he moved. I watched in amazement at first then noted what appeared to be big red pinchers on its tail.

That's when it I realised it might have been about to attack me. Suddenly the warrior in me took over again, and in one quick movement I got the broom and pushed it along the floor to the drain in the middle of the courtyard with the centipede going crazy trying to nip at the broom as he departed into the drainage system. Following this quest, I used the power of the internet to discover that it had a potentially fatal sting and should keep away at all costs. Well that was another valuable lesson learnt I thought as I cleared up the spoils before retreating into my little casa.

Rather than rushing out, I decided to make the most of being in the apartment and did a little pre-beach sunbathing. Instead of sea birds in the background, I could only hear the humming noise from the hornets who had angrily retreated up to the podium vines much to my discomfort, but I fell asleep in the sun happily knowing that they knew who was the boss and had learnt to keep their distance.

After creating my home cooked cuisine, my builder Rui turned up to look at some odd jobs. My trusted Google app struggled this time and almost asked Rui to install a complete new kitchen, so I asked Rui to return the next day with his English-speaking son.

That night I once again felt tired and decided to do the unthinkable: a bath in my unique little external bathroom and an early night.

When Rui arrived the next day, we went through the odd jobs and then had a little tour of the courtyard. Rui pointed out his previous quality works to his son, which he was very proud of. This reminded me of myself back home in London as I paced the cobbled streets pointing to roofs

I'd repaired while my son showed little interest as he sat in the front of my car seat switching between apps on his mobile phone.

Following my recent altercation with the angry scorpion disguised as a centipede, I decided not to tempt fate by stirring up the hornets' nest. I ventured out to the unspoilt beaches of Porto Covo, which sit quietly on the west coast just north of Milfontes, and based on the fact it's quite isolated I considered it somewhere I couldn't get myself in trouble by coming across any angry predators of nature.

As the church bells chimed at 9.36 for no reason, I gathered my belongings, and did inventory check of my beach bag. I gently closed the solid timber antique door behind me, hoping it would be a quiet day.

19. Porto Covo Beach Day

The roads were empty as expected with the odd car and lorry going about their everyday life. I was delighted to see investments had finally been made to repair the road surface. I arrived at Porto Covo town centre and the first thing I saw was a huge crane; it was clear that developers were moving in to expand the small cliff edge town. It's a shame but at least it would encourage more tourists, more investment and create much needed work for the local people.

I made my way through the village, past the local shops and perched on a natural slate ledge. As I gazed out over the distant waters, a wave approached and hit the rocks with so much natural force the water was thrown up some twenty metres, getting me soaked. The locals found it quite amusing, which fully explained why they were on the next ledge up. I put this down to experience and went back to the car in search of dry fluffy towels while a puddle of water formed around my feet.

I decided to go for a coffee in a lovely café bar and then on to seek a nice sandy beach. It was high tide so I ventured away from the rocks to try to find the perfect beach that I had been so eager to find.

During my beach hopping adventure, I came across a lovely spot a bit further up coast. No pre-formed concrete paving slabs here, the paths were formed with thick slabs of natural slate. After five minutes of taking in the stunning view, I continued up coast a little further to see what other hidden gems there were.

I came across a more distant section of the rock face and heard a thunderous roar as the Atlantic came crashing into the rocks with unprecedented force, sending the sea up into the clear blue sky. I climbed down the rock face to get a closer look, while the fishing boats tinkered with their nets in the distance in the hope of a good catch. I had my very own secluded beach, apart from the odd ramblers who would suddenly appear on top of the cliffs to take photos of this vibrant stretch of coastline.

After a few hours, the tide went out and I walked back to civilisation following the coast further north towards Sines. It was no surprise to be confronted by a naturist beach, although it still shocked me a little possibly because I was the only one who had any clothes on, but it this was a lovely beauty spot as well. I sat down for a bit, admired the stunning coastline and drank loads of water, but then remembered the banana in the bag I was sitting on. I felt a little uncomfortable eating a banana with naturists possibly watching, so I made my way back south to Porto Covo to laze on the sun drenched golden sands for the rest of day.

After a number of hours in the sun, I managed to wake myself up by my snoring echoing against the rocks. With so many advertising boards promoting McDonald's, I drove into Sines for a thick creamy milkshake. I didn't use satellite navigation system for the trip; I much preferred to get lost and take in the unexpected sites. I came across a castle, huge industrial areas, satellite and radar facilities and quite a few roads to nowhere. They simply ended for no apparent reason, which you get used to in Portugal. It's no doubt all part of their plan for future development.

After eating my food and indulging in a welcomed session of free Wi-Fi I got back into my car and drove down to the stunning marina. It had a bright orange glow as the sunset started to take hold, and I discovered a tower of natural sandstone rock with steps cut into the face leading to a viewing platform. What an amazing way to sit and watch the sunset.

By the time I got back to Santiago, it was dark. Then I realised that I'd forgotten to get my shopping, which was the main reason I'd travelled north towards the shopping district in Sines.

20. Best Kept Secret

I decided have a quiet day with a visit to my local BPI bank in Milfontes, but like all my plans it took an unexpected diversion while driving along the road that cuts through the Alentejo hills.

Out of the corner of my eye, I noticed a little dirt track cutting through the forest. At the last minute, I decided on a full wheel lock almost skidding into the shingle ditch at the side of the track. As I drove, all I could see in my mirror was a cloud of dust, which seemed to go on for miles. Luckily, the road ended at a complex so I stopped to explore further. I spotted a large set of bi-fold doors that led to an extremely large dining area and open country kitchen. People were preparing fresh food in huge cooking pots on the large traditional gas stove.

As I entered this fine art inspired building, I had a strange feeling of being transported into a fantasy world. I wandered into the farmhouse kitchen area of Herdade da Matinha and as I greeted the staff, I learnt that it was a health farm and hotel complex complete with animals.

The ladies were working extremely hard over the hot stoves on a sweltering day preparing fresh jams from locally grown tomatoes. Unfortunately they didn't speak English so called out to a young lady called Carla. She spoke perfect English and walked out with an amazing burst of passion and energy welcoming me to this fine establishment. I was instantly made to feel at home in this lovely country lodge.

She explained that guests could go horse riding through the unpopulated forests, which included paths leading to the golden beaches, and younger children are encouraged to help in the stables. They also offer yoga, rambling over the magnificent hills and through the wild green forests, chill out and DVD areas for the kids and a separate area for the adults. If that wasn't enough, they also have an amazing restaurant overlooking the farmhouse kitchen to let guests see the food fresh being prepared and cooked.

They gave me a tour and I was blown away by the place. It had fruit trees dotted around the landscape, sun loungers outside the brightly coloured lodges, a stunning swimming pool and loads more animals and wildlife to keep the little ones busy. Not surprisingly, it was created by a fairly well-known local artist and every part of the complex demonstrated this. The vibrant designs brought a creative energy to the place, which certainly rubbed off on Carla and the rest of the staff working in the kitchen. They were all so passionate and welcoming as I took photo after photo.

Walking around the various rooms was like walking into some sort of dream. The designs ranged from a quaint little historic coach house in the old quarter to a stunning open plan luxurious apartment.

Before leaving, I was taken to the kitchen to sample the tomato and fig jams, which were being made. They both tasted divine. I was invited to join the staff the following day for an authentic Alentejo inspired jam-making workshop.

Driving back into town the energetic atmosphere of the summer holidays was replaced by a much slower pace of life, and I headed straight to my bank. They were so helpful going out of their way to assist me, as did the local ice cream parlour and snack bar; by now, I was seen as a regular due to my previous trips.

Next I visited the local fishing tackle shop where I was given advice on bait and fishing in Alentejo. I finished with a cup of coffee up on the cliff top overlooking a fishing marina.

I decided to skip the beach and headed to the local butchers and supermarket intent on cooking my own Alentejo inspired BBQ with the finest ingredients including Parma ham, black olives, sweet Portuguese bread, quality black pork and the most succulent chicken breast topped off with a few slices of fresh pineapple. After getting back, cooking and scoffing my abundance of food I was left full and ready for a night of total relaxation, looking forward to a fishing trip to my secret lake, which only a handful of locals knew about.

21. Secret Pond

My alarm went off at the crack of dawn, and I struggled to get up and out as planned. I settled for slowly waking up prior to gathering my newly acquired fishing gear and heading out of the door.

Not quite remembering where the lake was. I took potluck and headed down the first dirt track that I came across. Arriving at the lake was quite a special moment as sheep were drinking the clear water from the lake and wandering around without a care in the world.

With my newly found knowledge of nature, the first thing I did was to check the area to ensure I wasn't caught out by any unforeseen surprises such as ants nests, venomous centipedes or any other predator. I kept a large rock by my side in case I happened to come across a wild bear or tiger and upon reflection this was perhaps a little over cautious. I rolled a few rocks over to double check for life and, sure enough, I found a good looking little fellow in the form of a lizard-like reptile, which scurried away after a few playful nudges with a stick into the safety of the long straw-like grass.

The lake was a good metre below the water line because of the severe lack of rainfall over the year, but still I could hear and see that the water was teaming with life. After an hour or so I came to the conclusion that sweetcorn might not be their most favourite dish, so I changed tactics and switched to the most horrible looking worms I'd ever seen, and cast out my size eight into the depths of the lake.

While waiting for my dinner, I decided to have a little paddle to cool down. Within seconds while I was standing on the water's edge up to my shins, I clocked some movement not far from me and saw a large freshwater lobster scurrying with its pinchers open towards my feet. I screamed out in horror, jumped out of the water and landed on my pot of worms, which were now slithering their way to freedom. Clearly, once again, this was not my finest hour.

After settling back down I noticed loads of small lobsters, which I assumed were crayfish, walking back and forth along the shallow depths of the water's edge. My friend Giovani wasn't joking when he said don't eat the lobsters, but with their massive claws I could guarantee that wouldn't happen.

After some time I got my first bite, which was unfortunate because I was unprepared and the fish managed to escape from my barbless hooks. I loaded on another worm, but was surprised by a sheep jumping out of the bushes near to where I was camped. Laughing aloud across the valley, I carried on in my quest and launched another worm at speed into the now busy lake.

It was idyllic sitting there listening to the chorus of lambs calling out across the water and into the valleys, the birds were singing happily and the occasional lobster scurried past me along the shallow waters. Swallows and metallic blue dragonflies hovered in and out of the long weeds into the cool breeze drifting through the valleys.

At 12.30 it must have been lunchtime for the fish; the tranquil lake became a hive of activity with fish constantly jumping and skimming along the surface. I watched my bait disappear and in the distance herds of sheep and goats were retreating up into the Alentejo hills. I walked around the lake to the adjacent field where I managed to get close enough to stroke the little lambs, which came inquisitively to greet me no doubt also looking for an offering of food.

I sat, waited and watched as the surge in activity was replaced with a total calmness. Every now and then, there was a loud splash as a fish displaced itself out of the water determined to catch the beautiful dragonflies that hovered above. But this time I was starting to feel quite drained and craving a ham toasty so I headed back to the car, along the little dirt track around the lake and over the hills leaving a trail of dust as I went.

There was some sort of monument across the field so I parked and walked to have a closer look. Water was cascading from the rocks into a little pool; I assumed this was viewed as a shrine to God to provide water as there were flowers left in front of it as an offering of thanks.

I drove back to my little casa for a treat of omelette, Parma ham, local sweet bread, pineapple and black olives. Time for a little siesta prior to a quick bath. That night I rustled up a quick dish using the tomato jam from those lovely people at Herdade da Matinha and, following my quick consumption, I headed out for a night time drive. I visited the delightful little town of Ourique then the historically interesting town of Castro Verde, which had a vibrant buzz in the air as people dined in one of the many rustic restaurants.

After another long day, I arrived back in Vale de Santiago intent on finally going to chill out in one of the local bars. On the one day I chose to sample some of the gorgeous locally produced port, my excitement diminished as I discovered they were all locked and bolted with no soul in sight. I settled for an early night as the clock struck ten in order to be up nice and early for a quick trip to wander along the gravel banks of river Mira in Odemira.

22. Shellfish Gold

Next day I was up early and ventured to the gorgeous town of Odemira. I parked and walked along the bank of the Mira below the amazing architecture of the curved white footbridge. Further down below the large red Victorian inspired bridge, I discovered a place of pure relaxation with a small table and chairs carved out of locally felled timber logs. I sat and listened to the birds, rustling leaves and chickens calling out to the dogs who were barking relentlessly with an odd lamb rising to make its voice heard; after all it was Election Day in Portugal.

After about an hour, I made my way to the restaurant/snack bar in search of a large white coffee and a custard tarte. I sat watching locals come and go with the ladies cuddling and kissing the little children and an elderly couple walking along holding hands adoringly. Most of the locals were smiling and laughing while they enjoyed the brilliant sunshine. This must be one of the happiest places to live.

It was then back to the car to head towards the various beaches dotted along the west coast, and I skilfully navigated the old red single lane bridge, which crosses the sensational Mira River. I arrived once again the aptly named Restaurante Oásis, which came with free Wi-Fi and its own decked area extending directly out onto the beach. I consumed more refreshments before making my way along the beach in pursuit of total relaxation with only the gentle sound of the waves to keep me occupied.

As I walked along the beach, I noticed stones piled high, so I placed one stone on top for good luck, adhering to local folk-law. After previously querying this strange ritual, I was lucky enough to meet a nun who sat down next to me in Milfontes to explain that if you see a rockfall it's customary to place a rock on top of the pile with the top rock pointing to the direction of your travels. This would bring you good luck and good fortune on your travels. She gazed into my eyes and said, 'Mr Englishman, did you know you have a special aura about you? Did you know you have spiritual guides?' With that, she said her farewell and retreated to the nearby convent.

It was a slightly odd thing to hear but she may have been right because I'd managed to become a born again domestic god, turning on my washing machine and tumble drier, and producing some great authentic Portuguese dishes. I felt like I had joined the ranks of the modern man.

I found a nice spot, not too isolated but close enough to be near others chillaxing in the midday sun. At the end of the day, I glanced around and noticed the water had receded, leaving amazing mud flats and people were appearing from all directions, digging with their bare hands. I packed my kit into the car and made my way over to them.

'*Olá*, you speak English?' I said in my polite little voice and I got exactly the response I anticipated.

'A little.'

'What are you searching for?' I asked.

'Sir, we are searching for cockles, I think you call them in England. If we don't find them we don't eat.'

I wished them good luck and walked further down only to discover another five or six people searching frantically for this shellfish gold. I trudged off down the beach looking for driftwood for my little bathroom, but for the first time ever I left the beach empty handed. I headed off in search of a great restaurant and stumbled across one of my favourite places in Milfontes, Paparoca's, adjacent to the historic fort, which sits proudly on the cliffs' edge.

After receiving great service and lovely food, I slowly wandered along the promenade. As I got to the end of the coastal road I was met with a beautiful sunset. I sat perched on the cliffs' edge with the other tourists and watched in awe at the amazing depth of colour that formed until it eventually disappeared beyond the horizon leaving us with only the twinkling stars and crescent shaped moon to light up the cobbled streets.

Driving down the dark country roads close to my village, I saw little eyes peering at me, which seemed to be startled by my headlights. I feared it might be the dreaded wild boar that I'd heard so many horror stories about, but fortunately there were two fluffy sheep busy grazing on the rounded grass banks, watching me closely while they munched on their supper.

As I got closer to my little casa, there was a hive of activity with loads of people shouting, dancing and singing along with a parade of cars repeatedly honking their horns. I remembered it was the local elections and the whole place had changed from a chilled-out, calm and laid backed atmosphere to an intense crazy election frenzy taking hold of the village. An army of people were driving around in the pursuit of votes; it certainly beat the door-to-door canvasing we're used to in England. Back home I rested my weary head on my soft fluffy pillows ready for a good night's sleep, however, the hooters started up again and the convoy was right outside my door. I quickly gathered up my video recorder and rushed to film the show. What a noise; then within no time at all it was silent and calmness was restored at 10.30 and 22 seconds.

Next day I rose early all bright eyed and bushy tailed, wondering what the day's events would bring. I was planning a super quiet day away from touring the country in search of new treasures.

I heard a tinkering of bells and it sounded as if the goats were outside my door. So I wandered to my little car, which was parked around the corner, and I was delighted to see an entire herd of sheep grazing on the dried up leaves that had fallen from the fig and pomegranate trees from the neighbouring garden.

Luckily, my video camera was in my pocket so I filmed them they as they grazed, totally oblivious to the fact I was there. I rushed back to get my mobile to snap some great shots, but upon my return they spotted me and made a quick getaway, the smallest one slow to react. It noticed my scary face then raced to off to catch up with the rest of his fluffy friends while the sound of their bells echoed through the valleys. As a bonus they had also given my car a buff with their fluffy coats.

23. DIY Day

After touring, chillaxing and eating loads it was time to do a little hard graft in terms of DIY. I spoiled myself with a home cooked breakfast, piling on the pounds in the process.

The boiler was first on the list of things to do as it had been playing up since the day I'd bought the place. I stripped it down, worked out how it operated with the heat exchanger and spark ignition, then hey presto! I noticed there was no electrical supply, something that had previously escaped my attention. I took a deep breath, removed the casing and staring me straight in the face was a leaking battery that had damaged the terminals. How could I fix it without calling my dependable builder, Rui, back without me looking like a lemon? Then I remembered I'd once made an electrical charge using a lemon; the only thing I had left in the kitchen was a lemon. I wondered if a battery ran out of power and in turn leaked acid, would lemon on the circuits possibly reverse this effect. I had nothing to lose, so I cut open one of my freshly picked lemons, squeezed the juice into a cup and dropped the component into it. There appeared to be some sort of activity. When I removed the part, I was extremely pleased to see that my plan had worked; the acid had been cleaned from the component and I managed to repair the boiler. I was getting good at village life, learning to adapt to any task and becoming as self-sufficient as possible, so decided to tackle all the electrics next while I was on a roll. How hard could it be?

I dissembled the sockets and lights while removing the sections of ceiling in order to carry out my upgrade. I worked hard to ensure I was able to complete the task; the children wouldn't be happy coming into a room with no light. I had no choice but to succeed, albeit with a call to my father back in London, Bombardier John, who was probably perched on his throne sampling the delights that the Pelton Arms in Greenwich had to offer. I decided to take a slight guess on the electrical configuration due to a lack of knowledge and took a total gamble before the day ended. After all fifteen or so repairs were carried out, I took a deep breath, hit the switch and in one massive burst of energy all lights and electrical fittings came to life without a hitch, and, more importantly, without any explosion or personal injury. After fixing an electrical radiator, running a few extension cables and filling a handful of holes to the authentic antique decorated walls I had a break before the task of cleaning my entire casa.

As I started the real hard graft, I managed to trip over cutting the back of my leg quite badly with blood pouring onto the ceramic tiles, which I had just cleaned. I went to get another much-earned drink and tripped over the large antique marble threshold, stubbing my little toe quite badly. Before I finished my cleaning, I also managed to drop a cabinet on my little finger, which by this point really tested me so I took a deep breath, manned up and continued my cleaning duties through to the end. I looked at the finished article with a sense of pride and achievement. It was now time to march round to Celeste in the local supermarket to gather my ingredients to rustle up a traditional Portuguese dish of pork, potato and carrots marinated in a red wine and red pepper sauce with a few slices of sweet Alentejo bread. Once again, I impressed myself as it ended up being the best meal I'd ever cooked, all thanks to my young chef friend Giovani who had inspired me to try to cook on my previous visit to his oasis of a garden in the valleys.

After consuming my large hearty meal and finishing off my Italian ice cream, I downed an entire litre of the finest water you could buy and chilled out listening to my newly acquired radio.

I reflected on my time deep in the Alentejo plains, and the fantastic people I'd met. All in all, this trip had been an incredible journey and never had my property purchase seemed such a bargain; the experience got better and better as I embarked on my travels of self-discovery.

The following day I would have one more beach day without any disruptions. I wanted to continue my self-discovery back on the coastal region and decided to go to one of my favourite quiet spots on Furnas Beach, which was a perfect end to get me ready for the hustle and bustle of city life again.

What I'd learnt on this latest adventure was that to make a dream come true takes hard work, passion and determination.

24. Final Beach Day

Before heading out it was time to skilfully progress my cleaning duties, which I now had down to a fine art. After two hours, it was job done and I headed out towards Milfontes, across the stunning bridge that passes above the fast flowing Mira River and down through the protected national park land picking up the little dusty dirt tracks, zigzagging my way down to my favourite section on Furnas Beach for a lovely peaceful rest.

This time I was equipped with my new cooler bag, the entire contents of my fridge/freezer and around four litres of juice. I also had a large bag full to the brim of things I might possibly need, which also made a fantastic pillow.

I found a lovely little spot right on the corner of some tidal flats on a patch of soft golden sand adjacent to the car, away from any people.

As I set up camp, I inhaled fresh sea air while listening to the sounds of nature. I applied my sun creams and oils, then just as I lay down a few cars turned up and the habitants jumped out to join me on my little isolated beach; my peace became a distant thought.

First to arrive was a local couple who were equipped with an expensive looking paddleboard and an even more impressive large, excitable dog who managed to completely disrupt the peace for a few hours. I decided to share the last of my food and walked over to the dog with a handful of Parma ham, which judging by his wagging tail was a welcomed treat. I had a little play with him while his male owner got on the paddleboard, making his way up river towards the stunningly designed Mira New Bridge, while his partner topped up her rich golden tan.

After a while, the dog's owner returned, much to the delight of the large fluffy dog, who was by this point barking loudly and wagging his tail. Eventually, around lunchtime, they packed up and quickly set off no doubt in search of great food in some local snack bar.

Finally it was time for some quality relaxation on my own, when I heard another car followed by a second car and out jumped a number of excitable English-speaking expats. My day's plan had failed badly.

The first lady who shimmied past me in the sand was an elegant older lady all dainty and perfectly dressed in her beachwear with a matching small beach bag neatly hanging from her shoulders. She was followed by a much younger larger than life character call Danny who came loaded with bags and other beach items and spoke extremely loudly. He sounded like an Essex car salesman with an odd twist of Black Country accent creeping into every sentence, which I found slightly amusing.

He came equipped with a large paddleboard, and I felt like a poorly equipped Englishman without one of my own. I sat and watched him as he attempted to get his big frame up onto the board, but unfortunately for him this was quickly followed by a head over heels back into the water. I was sure it would soon return to the peaceful and tranquil beach when he eventually got going, but as he made his way up river, he struggled to stay on the board time and time again, simply going round in circles.

He certainly had all the gear but no idea, as he attempted to get floating out towards middle of the river but he simply kept going round in circles much to the amusement of his older lady friend. She was yelling over to him while he shouted back to her, constantly falling off under the power of the swirls, his laughter bellowing out towards my eardrums.

When he finally made his way back to the shore, I congratulated him on entertaining me for the last hour. He introduced himself as Danny Boy as he trudged back to his lady friend for a spot of lunch and a glass of vino. At this point the peace almost returned until another car full of people arrived honking its horn erratically as they shouted over to Danny Boy and his elegant lady friend. It was clear that with Paddle Boy Dan and his accomplices, I wasn't going get that desired relaxing beach day, although talking to them and listening to the constant jokes and chuckles coming from their direction was at least quite entertaining.

After lunch, Danny Boy returned to the water and this time I could see a much improved and focused paddle boarder, and I couldn't resist telling him so. He had gained more confidence headed out much further to the middle of the Mira, getting a little help by the turn of the tide.

When he came back to the beach, he walked up to me, looked me in the eye and asked if I would like to try it. Eager to show my masculine competitive nature I took on the challenge. By luck more than skill, I jumped straight onto the dreaded paddleboard where Dan took great delight in strapping my leg to the safety rope. That's when it suddenly dawned on me. I could barely swim but before I knew it, I was on the board, floating out into the distance, struggling to stay afloat. I struggled to control the board, being careful not to show my fear to Dan who assumed I had a natural talent, no doubt.

I managed to stay on my feet as I battled the Mira swirls much to Dan's dismay, but, after a little water therapy, I decided it was actually quite hard work and returned the floater back to Dan, quite proud that it was in one piece. I think all the group were quite impressed that I'd managed to stay on two feet but there was definitely a hint of sarcasm as I gave it back. I then returned to the comfort of my private spot, gasping for water.

After a little while, Dan set off on the paddleboard again and found himself pulled right out to the bridge. I lay my tired head down and gently closed my eyes, repeatedly waking myself up by snoring. It seemed that I had become the entertainment much to my embarrassment, but I felt completely relaxed and ready for my return home early the next morning.

Eventually after a bit more time I got up and loaded my bags into the car for my final trip back through the brilliant countryside to my lovely little tranquil village. I wished I could just have had one complete week of rest and relaxation, but that time will come.

Every trip to the Alentejo seemed to get better and better and it was hard not to feel a little irritated at the thought of driving back home again the next day. But it was an amazing feeling knowing that I could simply travel out whenever I wanted.

25. Alentejo Reflections

I was at the airport waiting to board my flight home, reflecting on my time in Portugal so far. I couldn't help smiling about the fact that I was lucky enough to experience the majestic beauty of the Alentejo region and not just the typical Algarve club holiday experience. I sank back into super relaxed mode thinking about the unspoilt sandy beaches overlooked by the rich coloured sandstone and slate faced cliffs, while the powerful Atlantic Ocean stretched out to the distant horizon.

I found myself thinking about how lucky I was to have met people from the local population who commonly struggle to make ends meet but remain generally happy and content with their simple lifestyle. There was always a constant buzz and they were some of the friendliest people I'd ever met, which is something that we in the big cities could all learn from.

It was an odd experience the first moment I came across the village, driving past snack bars one after the other with villagers siting around watching a strange person coming into their lovely little community. It was amazing how quickly they accepted and welcomed me and this really added to the fun. No doubt a few patriotic individuals would be against foreigners setting up camp in their backyard. But deep down they must realise the alternative would be a major decline in the area.

Back home as the temperature dropped in the UK, and fireworks were bursting into life, I realised it had been a whole year since I took full ownership of the property on

5 November. Despite the cold, I still held a warm feeling inside knowing that I could go back to the village whenever I wanted. In that one year I had experienced a completely different way of life, slotting into the local community, battling with large centipedes, undertaking various professional DIY tasks and even learning how to navigate the Mira River without drowning, which was certainly a bonus.

With every experience, my mind became fragmented then pieced back together, which in turn changed me as a person. I genuinely appreciated the help that the people gave me, and I became willing to go that extra mile to help others as well. I started to respect nature, including its amazing wildlife such as Lenny the lizard or the huge slithering centipedes. It made me think about the environment and I started to adopt an approach to save and protect all natural resources, including a smarter use of water and recycling or refurbishing where possible rather than disposing of perfectly good items.

In my everyday day quest for knowledge of current affairs around the world, I no longer Googled the local news but preferred to explore further and deeper into Portugal, remaining extremely positive about the country's future. So much investment is trickling into the country, setting it up as a great place to invest, attracting Russians, Chinese, French and even Americans to take advantage of the attractive benefits it has to offer. Even the queen of pop, Madonna, decided to by a palace high up in the stunning tree-lined mountains of Sintra; even I didn't see that one coming!

With any positive, there's a negative, and I kept a close eye on the fires that affected the regions through Portugal. It was one thing that I hadn't considered when purchasing my property, but this area within the Alentejo is one of the safest regions.

During the first year, there were huge leaps in technology such as earphones available from our Google friends that listen to conversations then translate them into English. Having this technology on my mobile and taking the time to communicate in their language helped me to build and form relationships such as when I ordered my coffee in the brilliant O Tarro snack bar and restaurant in Odemira.

For the past eight years, I'd struggled annually with a chest infection as the cold weather drifted in. This year I really seemed to have escaped it, which I put down to diet, exercise and generally a feel-good feeling. It was amazing to know that I could simply fly out to my sun-soaked village, deep in the valley of Santiago. I'd proved that you don't need to be rich for this to happen; I've managed it with such a small investment and it has definitely been a life-changing period in my life. Well worth the investment.

Gone are the days of trudging along to my local football club, Charlton, shuffling along Floyd Road while scratching my head in disbelief at the poor results, prior to drowning my sorrows in the local establishments with a beer or two. I found that this life has been replaced by a much more simple and enjoyable life a world away from the hustle and bustle.

26. The Short One

Sitting in my office in Clapham one Thursday, I started to get itchy feet as I studied the latest property data coming out of the country. In Lisbon alone there had been a 36.92% increase in the property values in one year, which was simply mind boggling. This would create a ripple in the property values spreading out to the Alentejo regions, and prices will be further increased from the ripples also spreading from the Algarve region, which is also receiving massive investments. This made it a high gain potential, but with exceptionally low risks.

I started thinking about my next trip, imagining myself hiking out into the midday sun, rambling along the dusty tracks. I was now focused on my continued quest to explore other unknown areas, and at this point I was getting itchy feet. I needed another holiday to take in some more thought provoking and creative influences, along with a few glasses of local port and a few cold beers of course. I booked my flight for the next day.

Finishing work on a Friday in November temperatures, I was looking forward to popping over to Portugal with my daughter for a little sun to perk me up before the harsh winter months leading up to Christmas. I couldn't wait to indulge in my newly developed craving of a traditional baked custard tarte.

We had an early morning flight up into the stormy skies through thick grey clouds until we got close to the Algarve. There was a break in the clouds over the Alentejo with the sunshine reflecting off the previously dry lakes and rivers now filled with water.

As made our way through the empty airport in search of a fantastic hire car deal. We decided to treat ourselves to an upgrade this time as we were only there for a few days, so we went for a sporty looking Audi ready for powering up the through the Monchique mountains.

We had a quick pit stop in the new Ikea in Loule and poked our heads in the shopping centre that had just opened, gathering a variety of cheap t-shirts and shorts. By 11 a.m. we were on our way towards the peaks of the Monchique mountains. We found a large snack bar/restaurant complete with a battalion of firefighters tucking into an early lunch in the sunshine. After a little light refreshment, we set off up through the Algarve mountains then down towards the Alentejo, eager to get to the village and catch up with Celeste in the local supermarket before it closed. Then I remembered it was already siesta time so we stopped at a few local snack bars, entertaining the locals as we attempted to speak Portuguese. We gave in each time, relying on our best friend Google to help us. I didn't bother with satnav, opting to bring us an element of excitement as we passed some great sights through new terrain.

We arrived in Vale de Santiago just as Celeste was opening the doors with Alfonso assisting her with the gas bottle orders. They both greeted us as we arrived in search of the wet stuff while the locals queued up all eager to purchase their day's shopping.

After Ruby had finished soaking up loads of cuddles and squeezes, we made our way to the sanctuary of my little casa and headed straight to my garden podium. There was an abundance of grapes but unfortunately for us they were splattered all over the floor, resembling a murder scene. The tiles had become ingrained with dark red grape juice, another unforeseen task prior to a little relaxation. Ruby went to her bedroom in search of pencils and paper, leaving me to clear up the mess watched over by a few hornet wasps and Lenny the lizard who had happily come out to greet me like an excited pet dog but less of a wagging tail.

Once I'd finished cleaning, we fired up the charcoal and got cooking our matured aged meat and corn fed chicken, which we ate on the podium overlooking the fields surrounded by farm animals singing out in the background. This instantly transported us far away from civilisation. By the time we'd eaten, it was starting to get dark, so we quickly cleared up and went for a little drive out in to the valleys, returning some time later eager to rest our tired heads and we both collapsed on the bed instantly falling into a deep sleep. We woke up at dawn to the sound of cockerels and the animals scurrying around eager to hoover up the last of the fruits that had fallen from the trees scattered around the hills.

We grabbed breakfast and Ruby let me know that the milk tasted funny, the cornflakes were different and the juice had an odd colour. She decided she wasn't hungry and went to her room to get dressed where she had a secret stash of Jaffa cakes nestled on top of her little antique table.

'Busted,' I shouted as I burst through the door only for her Ninja instincts to kick in. She ran towards me like a scorpion seeking out its prey, stamping on my foot, sending me tumbling to the ground but not before dragging my Ikea wardrobe with me, causing it to break in half leaving yet another unforeseen repair task.

After we'd finished laughing, she helped me to my feet, gave me a cuddle and asked, 'Where are we going today?'

We got dressed and were off once again through the valleys, over the hills, down dirt tracks until we arrived in Milfontes, and made our way straight to the stunning beach eager to cool down by splashing in the blue water. It seemed to be calling out to us to join it and in we went prior to a few games of tennis, followed by a little football and a game of catch. The locals walked past in their tight jeans and thick woolly jumpers watching us play around in our swimwear, no doubt thinking we were crazy English people.

Not many days after we flew back to Gatwick, but what a great start to the real winter months.

27. Pre-Christmas Tan

The weather was really starting to turn so I decided it was crucial to squeeze in another trip before Christmas, or Natal as my Portuguese friends called it.

Looking through the offers on my site, I discovered flights in December had dropped to an unbelievable £17.99. Without hesitation, I decided to book another sneaky little trip where I hoped it would still be warm. Unfortunately, Samantha partner was a little busy so once again I was forced to go alone.

Getting on the plane after struggling to escape from the endless layers of weather protection, to the amusement of the elderly lady sitting close by, I was comfy and ready for the latest phase of my journey with no plans this time.

As we headed over the country, it was quite overcast again, but as we crossed over the Sintra Mountains and above Lisbon, or Lisboa as I now refer to it, I was extremely pleased to see the sunshine appearing through the thick broken clouds. They got thinner and thinner as we flew over the Alentejo region and as we landed the clouds had been replaced by deep blue skies.

This time I decided to go slightly off track, and instead of visiting my usual haunts I wanted to attempt a slightly different approach to prevent me getting stuck in a rut. So, I took a completely new route up through the Algarve mountains. Along the way, I was so happy to see that the water had completely returned to the previously dry riverbeds and they were now bursting at the seams and hopefully ready to sustain a plentiful supply of quality river fish.

I made the gradual climb up the mountain roads, zigzagging my way up to Foia, the highest peak. I stopped at various vantage points to take in the stunning scenery, watching the wildlife come and go. Travelling further up the mountain, my head hurt slightly as the altitude caused the air to become thinner, and there was definitely a large temperature drop but it was still quite pleasant given the time of year. As I arrived at the peak, I was speechless as I looked out over the picturesque landscape, a mixture of lush green grass with patches of long straw-like grass with loose rocks dotted around.

As I wandered around, I discovered more mystical stones and rocks piled up on the mountain pass to symbolise visitors' spiritual connections to the earth and ancestors that watch over them. They formed some sort of sacred monument and an English-speaking young boy explained that showing this heartfelt respect brought you luck, while marking your path of travel. It was clear that the locals really believed this; it was common for individuals to make a pilgrimage up the peak and show their respect by placing some stones before their long descent back down.

I rested on a little rock, deep in thought, and failed to notice the extra-large bull that had become resident next to me. While he was busy grazing, I got up very slowly and sneaked away quietly to my car to seek out some well-earned refreshments. Lucky for me this was no fighting bull and I made my way to safety. Then I wandered over to a hilltop café prior to my onwards journey, but not before passing through the historical town centre of Monchique where there were some amazing natural sulpha springs with baths and spas in the middle of the forest with the background sound of running water, which was quite relaxing.

On my unscheduled diversion, I came to a little shop and a great little secret in the form of a local brew by the name of Medronho created from distilled Medronho berries. What an amazing taste it was. I was so grateful for the taste test I decided to by treat myself to six bottles, much to the delight of the nice lady serving but then remembered I would be unable to take them in the cabin on the plane so I would be forced to consume them myself.

The sun was still shining but it had been replaced by a more subtle sunshine, which served to promote that feel-good feeling before my return to the UK to prepare for Christmas.

It was a quiet week going to some of my usual haunts, but this time I took things a little easier and really enjoyed my simple little casa, which had now become home from home in this relatively unknown region in Portugal.

Again, before I knew it I found myself all too quickly arriving into UK airspace, but this gave me an incredible burst of energy leading up to Christmas. It would be a tough few months, spending my hard-earned money over the Christmas period, which would not doubt prevent me from undertaking my routine monthly dash to Portugal. Yes, it was becoming a bit of a habit, but an enjoyable one.

I'd learnt that in life we come with nothing and we go with nothing, but what often sets us apart from others is our ability to think as an individual and open our mind to a diverse way of thinking and in turn lead a more complete life.

28. The Unknown Tour

Shortly after Christmas, I couldn't resist another quick trip and off I went for a super-fast visit, just because I could. After picking up my car, I drove up the long winding roads through the mountains of dreams, but I came down through thick clouds and grey skies.

After getting to my village, I wanted to drive through unknown regions without any maps and simply follow my instincts.

I headed out, parked in the glorious sunshine, and trekked across the open plains and around the cone shaped hills and eventually came across some amazing colonial architecture. I wandered over to have a look and discovered this fine building had been empty for a long time; the large solid wood doors were ajar so I couldn't help feeling a little curious. It reminded me of the haunted houses you see in classic movies, but I couldn't resist having a little wander inside once I was satisfied the lonely little structure was definitely empty.

As I made my way through the creaky old doors surrounded by colonial pillars and detailed corbels, I was in awe at the traditionally cut timber staircase winding its way up through the building. It was hard to believe that the antique handcrafted ceramic tiles and oak panelled walls were still intact. I was surprised that this fine establishment hadn't been converted into some sort of stately home or hotel. I wandered in a little deeper, it was quite dark due to the shutters being shut, then I heard the sound of wild animals and barking dogs close by so decided make my way back to the car before being attacked by a ferocious pack of hungry dogs or worse.

After about an hour, I discovered a snack bar and popped in for some midday refreshments. Wow, did they go down well. Using Google Translate, I asked the locals about the house I'd just visited. They looked bemused and shook their heads almost dismissing the fact the house existed. I thought it was slightly odd so after downing a quick beer and a nice cool coke to bring up my sugar levels, I followed my route back to try to retrace my steps. It was impossible because everywhere looked the same so I made my way back to my little sleepy village.

Inspired by the produce of this rich diverse landscape I decided to prepare my latest culinary experience. I prepared a salad topped with a drizzle of olive oil and a sprinkling of locally produced goats' cheese accompanied by a plate of rich black olives.

Before I knew it, I was back at work following my quick weekend break.

29. Final Furlong

March was bitterly cold in the UK so I was delighted to be heading back to my little village in the heart of the Alentejo. I'd heard a whisper that there was a newly constructed designer village to check out. It was a superb development with not only the normal collection of outlet retailers but also a play park with underground caves, water features and children dashing around the marble floor tiles in electric cars dodging the endless bargain hunters who shuffled from one shop to another in search of great bargains.

After a few hours my hunger got the better of me so I got back on the road and took a trip to the Algarve coast and my favourite little area of Olhos de Agua. I found a super little restaurant with lovely staff and even better prices. I sat there consuming my food watching people wander down the hill to the promenade to enjoy the gorgeous view out across the Mediterranean Sea.

After another few hours, I was on the road and eager to get to my village. As I reached the Alentejo, I was shocked at the change of colour in this rich vibrant landscape. No longer were there field after field of rich golden grass. They had been replaced by rivers bursting at the seams along bright green banks, which had increased the activity of the grazing animals gently taking their time to chew on the fresh grass. The place had been transformed by the recent weather, but I couldn't help wondering if my little casa had withstood such heavy rainfall.

I needed to stock up on supplies so, knowing that the local supermarkets were unlikely to be open I drove into Ourique through a maze of little roads and discovered a huge Easter parade of some sort. Unfortunately I had no time to stop.

As I got closer to the village, I felt a little nervous hoping that the property hadn't been flooded. To my absolute delight it was all intact and as I opened the door I was pleased to discover it was in really good condition. Once again, there were signs of condensation so I would need to do a bit more planning before the next visit.

Rather than sitting down to recover from my 2.30 a.m. start, I set to work cleaning and then stupidly became engrossed in cutting down my grape vine and clearing up the mess. By the time I'd read my letters and completed the work I fell into bed and slept like a baby all night and I hadn't noticed that the church bells had failed to chime. Before I knew it was 9.30 and I just as I was waking up, Rui and Rui Jnr, my trusted builder friends, were ringing the doorbell.

Things finally appeared to be going to plan without any complications as we talked through my various minor work proposals. Rui asked me if I'd like to see his large complex project at the other side of the village, so I grabbed my mobile and my keys and off we went.

After a short drive through the quiet village, we passed the local cemetery and came to a fork in the two roads. Sitting proudly was a neglected property, which I had previously had my eye on, that turned out to be Rui and his team's next big project. It was already at quite an advanced stage of development. Gone were the cheap chipboard units, which were piled up in the garden for firewood, replaced by traditional cast concrete with ornate inset sinks with the concrete ready to be polished and sealed.

During the tour of the property, I learnt a lot about the Portuguese methods of building; quite a few of the buildings are constructed using a mix of earth. Apparently it's normal in Portugal although my house is built using tough tubular engineering type bricks, which will remain solid, but Rui reassured me, 'If it falls down don't worry we will rebuild for you, cheap.' We looked at the insulation in the roof, the plans for the pool and I was amazed at their passion and pride as they spoke; the quality of their work was outstanding and all for a relatively small sum of money. After some time analysing the project and materials, I had a little wander down the street to look at the neighbouring dwellings, but as ever I had work to do so it was time to go.

When I got back, I tried to unlock the front door, but my key failed to go in. That's when I realised that I'd rushed out without removing the internal key. I was stuck. Fortunately, however, I had a builder who could do anything, so I rushed down to seek assistance. Not for the first time, my dependable R&R gathered up their tools and ladders and came to my rescue.

Prior to climbing onto the roof, Rui senior pulled out a little foldable penknife. A few minutes later my dependable Rui became my saviour and after a few turns he managed to free the key from the lock – much to my relief.

I dashed off to a few little towns, first Colos to my little Chinese shop and then to Cercal in search for a boiler part. Unable to help, the people started making phone calls and people seemed to turn up from all over the town to assist me. Eventually the shop assistant asked me in her broken English to 'come back with me' much to the amusement of the young boy who was helping. She failed to see any issue with her chosen words, but I was happy to follow her to another shop in seek of additional help.

I went back home and decided to tackle trimming the grape vines with my new cutting gear. I'd only intended to spend an hour, but I finally finished and some four hours later the garden area was in a reasonable condition again, which wasn't easy due to the recent storms.

Rather than meeting up with Giovani, I decided on a night in and a few glasses of vino. Much to my annoyance, I realised that I didn't have any wine glasses. It was an odd experience drinking locally produced Alentejo wine in a cup, but it went down well anyway. I retired to my bed ready for the next day's challenges safe in the knowledge that I had no major tasks ahead and could start to enjoy the property with the thought of pure relaxation finally on the horizon after quiet a long year.

30. Crossroads

It was supposed to be a relaxing day, but I was starting to understand that I struggle to relax. My mind seemed to keep switching into hyper-mode, which sent me off to explore every inch of the local area in the quest for new knowledge.

I got up late, did a little more DIY and caught up with Giovani who assisted me in using the cash machine in the village. He arrived in style on a traditional looking motor bike complete with a dazzling chrome exhaust. He laughed at me wearing shorts; judging by the fact he was wearing layer after layer he obviously wasn't impressed with the winter sun, but I was making the most of it.

After a useful lesson in using a foreign cash machine, we both headed to Odemira. Giovani had an appointment and I wanted to visit my favourite snack bar for a coffee, coconut cake and freshly squeezed orange juice to wash it down.

Next I drove to my favourite Chinese shop adjacent to the Mira River and after a little expenditure I went for a gentle stroll along the riverbank. The sunshine radiated down on me and after a while, I could feel my head starting to burn so I walked back to the car and back along the riverbanks until I got to the café again.

All day the plan was to meet my trusted agent Tim and then go to the village to have a few drinks with my friends in their stunning little metropolis garden, but once again I got talking to a variety of people and the time passed by at great speed.

After another little adventure in the Milfontes Chinese shop where I broke two wine glasses while reaching up on the shelf, I left before I could do any more damage. In my quest to source boiler parts, the shop staff phoned around Portugal and requested that I return the next day. Was this the turning point where things would now go perfectly?

That evening sitting up on my quaint little podium, I watched the herons circling overhead along with all the other little birds flying around, chirping across the isolated valleys while the sheep and lambs grazed below on the fresh green grass. With the chickens and the peacocks to watch in the background with the sun setting over the hills, I felt a huge sense of achievement. I now had a perfectly habitable property awaiting my guests for the summer.

Looking around the village, however, it was clear that life was a real struggle for the locals. Many were unable to drive and there was a lack of decent employment opportunities, so for most the only means of making a living was to relocate to the big cities such as Lisbon, leaving behind a community crying out for people to help support the village infrastructure. The only hope would be for property investors from Lisbon or international buyers to sustain some form of balance to help the small local bars and traditional stores to remain open for the villagers to enjoy their simple life while at the same time increasing tourism.

It was time for a drive along the beautiful coast, so I headed into Porto Covo. I was shocked by the amount of ongoing development; this was a good indicator that locals were moving away from the inland communities, driving building growth along this inspiring coastline.

Just past Porto Covo I found a few little restaurants and decided to grab a coke. Just as the glass touched my dry lips, a young lady appeared and asked in English I was going to Sines. I quickly told her no and ushered her away. The waiter appeared and asked if everything was okay. I smiled, said yes and apologised for being a bit sharp with the young lady. I reflected on my actions as I sunk the ice-cold coke down my neck. Feeling guilty, I jumped into my car and drove her to Sines, which was only a ten-minute drive but a two-hour walk.

She told me that she had walked around the coast from Faro along the Algarve prior to making her way up the west coast, which equated to walking about 240 miles in total. This amazed me. I indicated that we both had something in common: I also liked to explore the only difference being I like to have four wheels and an engine.

Her name was Emilka and she came from Poland but had spent time living near Leeds in England prior to deciding to walk the entire length of Portugal alone. I asked her if she got scared, but she said she just feels a little apprehensive now and then. Sometimes she found hostels but mostly she was forced to camp somewhere secluded overnight to take shelter, but during the recent storms in Faro she was forced to seek sanctuary in a local church.

Eventually we arrived at the palm-lined promenade of Sines and I showed her the direction to take, wished her good luck on her travels along this amazing coastline and made my way back to my little sleepy village. I was totally inspired by Emilka's adventure, but I didn't think my partner would let me do such an amazing challenge for the next three months.

On the final day of this latest chapter in my life, I agreed to meet Tim in Milfontes for a coffee and light lunch, then see Giovani and his father for coffee in one of the two local snack bars. To my delight, I was informed that his father had bought a fresh crab and a speciality in the form of barnacles, which came all the way from Spain and they invited me back to their garden overlooking the Alentejo hills. That night, following quite a few glasses of the finest vino and another coffee, it was time to say goodbye. I retreated to my little casa after another amazing night in my friends' company. I couldn't wait to return.

I had met some incredible people and travelled to some truly wonderful coastal and inland towns, building up a huge amount of local knowledge and contacts in my time in the Alentejo. Now that my mission was complete, I couldn't help wondering if I should sell my wonderful little casa or spend a year or so of pure enjoyment. I was getting ideas for my next adventure as I cast my eyes over the estate agent's latest offerings; quite a few projects were starting to appear. I started to think about where my future would lie in the Alentejo, and I found myself at a crossroads of Alentejo emotions.

We will see.

All journeys in life have a beginning and an end but before you reach the end, life will throw a variety of challenges your way and unless you embrace that change you will not happily reach that finishing line content.

Acknowledgements

I also dedicate this book to my late friend Derek C (*Delboy*) who was a true inspiration to me and others, holding the belief that anything is possible. He brought guidance and constructive criticism in a unique way without which, this book would never have happened.

I would like to thank my brilliant Remax estate agent Tim, who was simply amazing and remains so.

Also a huge thank you to my ever dependable builder Rui Costa and his son Rui Costa *jnr* who is always on hand to assist me with my every need.

And gratitude to my young chef friend and his amazing family who were simply inspirational, due to their passion of freshly produced food and love of the simple village life.

Use others' doubt as a positive distraction to refocus your dreams in order to bring them to reality and the negativity becomes part of history.

Believe in your dreams! – Lee Middlenam

Helpful Tips

Should you be interested in following you own dream, you'll find a good few tips on buying in a foreign land.

- Create a list of requirements such as realistic amount of bedrooms, how close to the beach and how close to the airport. Two hours inland from Faro would get you some amazing bargain properties.
- Try to pick a spot between two airports – Alentejo sits near three: Faro, Beja and Lisbon.
- Be realistic on budget. No mortgage is great because you won't need to rent it out to cover the running costs. My little casa costs only 20 euros per year for council tax due to its location and size.
- Think about crime risks. Properties in the countryside and along the south-west coast see very little crime in Portugal compared to the tourist areas around the Algarve and major cities. But the risks are still minimal with Portugal being one of the safest countries in the world.
- Carry out fire risk reviews and look at the national fire maps.
- Ensure you have a designated water supply and electrical supply.
- Budget 10% for fees and don't forget how many trips abroad to finalise the deal will be required.
- Create a list of online properties and be willing to negotiate on a higher value one, in order to try and get the value reduced to your desired budget.
- If you pull out once the deal has been agreed and signed, you'll be liable for costs based on the

property value. If the seller pulls out, they'll be subject to higher costs, double the deposit.
- Check that your estate agent can put you in touch with local builders or, at the very least, get them to introduce you.
- Only use registered agents, unless you like a gamble. I went to the world renowned Remax network in Milfontes in the Alentejo region but there are loads more great independent agents out there.
- Ensure you have a good translator on standby for the Notary office and solicitors. Good agents will generally have an English or Dutch speaking person on standby.
- Most importantly, don't be put off by the negativity of others. It's normally a form of jealously so rise above it and be happy that you're following your dreams.

Helpful Links

Feel free to share in our experience we would love to hear from you. Please place My Little Casa in the subject and email the team at and you never know we may even assist you with a little local builder. lee.middlenam@gmail.com

A great place to start your search would be Rightmove. https://www.rightmove.co.uk/overseas-property/in-Portugal.html

To grab a real bargain visit Pure Portugal, you will be amazed. https://www.pureportugal.co.uk/

For a really great estate agent you can't get much better than the Remax team in Milfontes. https://www.remax.pt/1000

If you are looking for inspiration, a good start would be A Place in the Sun *live* - *https://www.aplaceinthesun.com/exhibitions*

Feel Free to hunt us down and follow us on Social Media and share us to the world!

Printed in Great Britain
by Amazon